LEARN TO LIVE

A System of Survival and Self-He

Stéphanie Spindler is a qualified and experienced teacher. She has an original approach based on a blend of her own personal experience and her professional expertise, which she uses to teach people to look at life in a different way. She gives specific and practical guidance to people which enables them to have choices in their lives. Stéphanie has worked at a private clinic in Beaconsfield for five years alongside a medical herbalist and an experienced nurse and her success rate is such that she only sees people on average a dozen times before they are able to go their own way.

Learn to Live

A SYSTEM OF SURVIVAL AND SELF-HELP

Stéphanie Spindler

E L E M E N T

Shaftesbury, Dorset • Rockport, Massachusetts

© Stéphanie Spindler 1991

Published in Great Britain in 1991 by
Element Books Limited
Longmead, Shaftesbury, Dorset

Published in the USA in 1991 by
Element, Inc
42 Broadway, Rockport, MA 01966

Designed by Roger Lightfoot
Cover design by Max Fairbrother and Barbara McGavin
Phototypeset by Intype, London
Printed and bound in Great Britain by
Billings Ltd, Hylton Road, Worcester

British Library Cataloguing in Publication Data
Spindler, Stéphanie
   Learn to live : a system of survival and
   self help.
   I. Title
   158.1

   ISBN 1–85230–298–4

Library of Congress Data Available

Dedicated to
John-Andrew

Foreword

This book by Stéphanie Spindler is relatively short and is an attempt to help people who do not feel at ease, who are aware that something is wrong with them or with a relationship which concerns them, and who cannot just 'put their finger on' the 'crunch' point. The author succeeds in guiding the reader through the elements of human beings – their thoughts, feelings, emotions and bodies in a positive and helpful way.

The introductory section is precisely written and 'sets the scene' for living. It introduces several basic concepts and encourages the reader to embark upon an exploration of several different, and maybe new, areas.

The first part of the book defines patterns of habits called types, and because there are elements of so many different types in all of us, the reader is implicitly challenged to seek out his or her type. The second section of the chapter explains our emotions of apathy, fear, anger, desire and pride; it contains some useful advice as well.

The second part has a section on exercise, which includes references to diet, sport, stress stagnation, breathing, together with another section entitled rest and relaxation which covers reasons for the inability to relax and the use of showers.

The third section of the book is entitled 'Waking Up To Your Internal World' and covers such topics as goals and dreams, listening within, love and death in a most interesting and informative way.

The major final section on visualization examines the power of the mind, making your own self-help tape, the psychology of self-perception and free will, and contains some first-class advice on making a new start, a new beginning. The coda too, encourages the reader to fight, and struggle, and battle towards self-realization.

The whole book is written in a straight-forward, very readable style, easy to comprehend, with good examples and an engaging approach which says in essence, 'What have you got to lose . . . why not try it?'

In my opinion, the book will be of great use to many people because they will welcome the lucid style, the authoritative statements and the open approach and it will enable them to take some action in the face of adversity. I expect the book to be used in several different ways. Some will use it as a text book or primer – following it section by section with a good break in between to work ideas and techniques through. Others will use it as a counselling book – to dip into when they or other people are in need; and still others, as I did, may feel that they want to read it through several times to explore every shade of meaning and every communicative message within the text.

It is amazing to find such a short book as this which

includes so many good ideas and so many sound strategies, all in such a concise, readable and easy format.

Dr Andrew Trott, A.C.P., Ad. Dip., M.Ed., F.C.P. (Hon), F.Coll.P.
The Dean, The College of Preceptors.
The President, European Institute for Vocational Training Commission on Technology-based Training.
Director, The Network of Evaluation and Training Specialists.
Vice President, The Association for Educational and Training Technology.

Contents

Acknowledgements

My thanks to all those who have helped and supported me and to those who have contributed to this book; they know who they are.

To Clive, my brother, who, with great patience, nurtured me back to life.

To my son Peter who, when 15, taught me that 'Desire is a trap and to be without Desire is liberation'.

To Abdullah Yusus Ali whose words of wisdom, reproduced overleaf mirror the pain and despair that brought me to the writing of this book.

Our life is subject to inner storms far more devastating than those in the physical world around us.

In such a storm, in the bitter anguish of a personal sorrow which nearly unseated my reason and made my life meaningless, I began to analyse and become aware of the forces at work which so blatantly pushed me to the brink of my own destruction.

Watered by many tears this manuscript was born as a system of survival and self-help.

Abdullah Yusus Ali

The Object of the Book

This book is meant for those who do not feel at ease. For those who work hard under stress and who cannot ease the pressure. For those who have lost touch with themselves, who wonder, 'Where did the person I thought I was go?' For those who find themselves boxed in and trapped. For those who feel they have lost control of their lives.

It is a book for those who cannot sleep well, who do not feel refreshed in the morning, who wake sluggish and lacking in vitality and whose bodies feel heavy and a burden.

It is a book for those who cannot shed fear and self-doubt to the exclusion of peace of mind, who seek to bring about change and don't know how.

The Game of Life

Living is participating in the game of life. In this game, few of us excel. This is mainly because we don't believe in our abilities, are not prepared to commit ourselves, or don't have the knowledge of how the game should be played.

When the 'slings and arrows of outrageous fortune' assail us through circumstances beyond our control we have three choices. We can decide to grow from the experience; we can walk out of the game; or we can become mere onlookers, choosing non-action.

Just as the athlete needs to learn to bring about a harmonious balance between the physical, mental and emotional parts of his being and accept certain disciplines within his life in order to give himself a chance to play his best game, so too can we learn about our strengths, our weaknesses and limitations and that it is all right to accept our limitations. Our lives are like an individually designed obstacle course and understanding each obstacle, having the know-how, being committed, disciplined and prepared to examine ourselves helps a great deal towards positive participation in the game of life.

How many times have you heard someone say, 'What you have to do is change your life'? Well most of us don't know how to bring about this change. For a start we just don't know ourselves. The inscription in the Temple at Delphi was, 'Know Yourself; then you will know the universe and the gods'.

It is hoped that the following chapters will answer some of your questions and give you the know-how to bring about the desired changes, ultimately putting you in control of the game of life rather than letting it control you.

Introduction

This book has four subject areas: our thoughts, our feelings and emotions, our bodies and our spirit – the four elements that make up a human being.

Of these, thought is in many ways potentially the most powerful as it can rule and control both the emotions and the body. It therefore follows that to achieve a state of emotional equilibrium, not subject to the destructive influence of negative feelings and physical debility, the mind as generator of thought must be understood and harnessed.

The mind comprises the conscious and the unconscious. The conscious is that part of the mind that interacts directly with the present time, aware of the information from the senses. It also receives images from the unconscious. The unconscious mind is like a photographic plate that records everything an individual sees or hears. Under deep hypnosis a subject can recall astonishing details from this storehouse.

It is important that negative thoughts and feelings be prevented from entering the unconscious. If we record fear, anxiety, insecurity, hate or intolerance, then this is what we draw on and this will colour all our thoughts, actions and speech. For as two things cannot occupy the same space, the conscious mind cannot think of two things simultaneously. If the mind is filled with

positive thoughts, negative ones cannot lodge there.
Positive, harmonious thoughts must be introduced into
the unconscious to replace negative ones, and so trans-
form it.

The unconscious is alive and continually changing
like the cells of our bodies. It is constantly being fed
by the experiences and feelings it receives from the
conscious mind. These experiences include all the
thoughts and feelings that are held strongly enough to
create an impression on the unconscious. The traumatic
experiences of childhood or the past, for example,
which have been felt with great intensity and fed into
the unconscious mind usually remain there and are not
replaced with new and more constructive impressions.

The impact of experiences, especially negative ones,
can be such that we create a defence mechanism that
sets our whole personality into a negative reaction
which stagnates our life and blocks change. This can
hold us in a negative circuit of behaviour and thought;
like a broken record it will dominate our hearing. We
have to learn how to undo the damage or ask for help.

The unconscious is the totality of a person's experience from birth until the present. Everything new that
enters into our consciousness changes it in the light
of the quality of the experience, whether negative or
positive. The more intense the experience, the more
lasting and prominent the impression will be on the
unconscious.

Our consciousness draws from the unconscious mind
the images and memories that relate to whatever is
acting upon it. If, for example, an experience of seeing
a certain person has always been painful, a proposed
meeting will draw the impressions relating to the pain
from the unconscious, and a feeling of dread will
accompany the thoughts of this person. However, a

proposed meeting with someone who loves us and has always been kind to us will trigger feelings of delight and pleasant anticipation as we recall happy times that we have spent with them. If someone who is accustomed to rejection overhears a conversation about a forthcoming marriage, this will probably launch them on to a painful train of thought.

It follows that, in order to live a life free of what is, in effect, negative programming, we need to understand the ways in which we can affect the unconscious and change what is in there and how it is reacting. It is also vital to realize that in the light of its programming, the unconscious acts largely out of habit. It does not discriminate, but only stores experience according to degrees of emotional impact, so that whatever situation we are in during our lives, the unconscious will recall related experiences from the past, selected in order of intensity. This fuels our emotional reactions and so makes it hard to change the way we behave unless we tackle the problem from the roots.

So:

A trigger event touches the conscious mind.
Unconscious programming relating to the trigger from past experience is drawn on.
We experience feelings about the trigger as emotions.

As this is part of every human's experience, examples can illustrate this by triggering your own memories.

Trigger	Letter from a close friend suggesting a picnic.
Unconscious reaction	What fun that will be.
Emotional reaction	Warmth, pleasant anticipation.

Trigger	Police come to front door.
Unconscious reaction	What have I done? Is someone I love in danger/trouble?
Emotional reaction	Fear, doubt, worry, anxiety.
Trigger	Late for meeting.
Unconscious reaction	They have done it before. I am inconvenienced. Intolerance.
Emotional reaction	Anger.
Trigger	Husband late home.
Unconscious reaction	Who is he with? I am neglected. My position is insecure – images from life, TV, books, and so on.
Emotional reaction	Anger, fear, jealousy.
Trigger	Colleague is praised for his work.
Unconscious reaction	I am better than he is.
Emotional reaction	Jealousy, pride.
Trigger	Newspaper story of widow's grief for her famous husband.
Unconscious reaction	Memory of loss of own husband, pain and loss.
Emotional reaction	Grief.
Trigger	Hearing a piece of music.
Unconscious reaction	Memory of lover who rejected you or, memory of beautiful evening of calm listening to the same piece.
Emotional reaction	Pain and grief or, calm, peace and love.

In order that we can rise above this limited state of conditioning where we are at the mercy of our unconscious, we have to use our will and the power of thought.

However, conditioning and habit create such a deep tangle of defences, blocks and emotions that we have to study them individually. In doing this, we learn to recognize the depth and processes of our negative programming and subsequent emotional reactions. We learn to combat and change them, thereby allowing new ideas and programming to take hold without our blocking them.

In so doing, we recognize the degree to which life is a learning process, 'an individually designed obstacle course' intended to lead us by our experience of suffering from our negative programming to a mastery of it. By replacing that negative programming with our objective thoughts and will, we can change our lives replacing doubt, fear, anger, pride, grief and apathy reactions with love, creativity, fulfilment, harmony and action.

PART ONE

Habits and Emotions

Learning About Our Habits

How do we fall into the traps that set habits into our natures? Why is it that one person reacts differently to another in the same circumstances?

One person will grasp an opportunity with enthusiasm, whereas another will recoil from the same chance with anxiety and fear. Their individual programming of experience will lead them to a different viewpoint of the world and circumstances.

● WHAT YOU ARE BORN WITH

There is a widespread belief that when we are born we are like a blank sheet of paper on which life begins to write. Alternatively, it is also considered that the period in which we are carried in our mother's womb begins the process of determining our nature.

That these nine months do affect us is well-documented. The physical changes brought about by drugs, alcohol and cigarettes used by a pregnant woman on her unborn child are distressingly obvious.

Experiences, mood and environment can also change the personality of an unborn child, just as the moods and attitudes of one person can affect someone else, purely by that person's presence. We all have the capacity to feel and how much more would an unborn child feel in its internal world, within its mother's body? Just consider how you would feel if you were locked up in a room with someone in a state of fear, anxiety, anger or grief for nine months!

However, there seems to be more to the formation of a child's personality at birth than these two viewpoints – that we are either born as a blank sheet or that the formation we have is via our mother, and begins prior to our birth.

Anyone who has been a parent or had much to do with family and children will have seen the discrepancies. Some children can have the attitudes and personalities of an adult in a small body, while others are angry, irritable, wise, calm or show personal traits that go beyond these two viewpoints.

It is as though each child has its own emotional nature and mind when it begins life – a uniqueness which exists beyond biology or the influence of parents and the environment, its own habits and conditioning from birth that set, to a degree, the pattern of its experiences and life. It is hard for science to verify such an idea as it is beyond its scope to understand certain aspects of the unborn personality. However, experience shows that a child is to a large extent its own person, with all the hang-ups of an adult.

The pattern of habits we either already have or go on to acquire can fall into types. These are essentially defence mechanisms we have learned to operate and in which we are stuck. Below are a few of the personality types which are the result of habit and conditioning. There are, of course, others, and most people have elements of several of these types in their nature.

● THE FEAR TYPE

Some of us are oversensitive by nature and for those of us who are like that, the world can seem a cold and hostile place into which we do not seem to fit. We know that we need to be loved but are afraid of rejection. This feeling of rejection is often deeply rooted in our childhood. We can feel anger, even rage, at our position but cannot express our feelings because we fear we will not be accepted; we will be further rejected.

But we should not retreat into our inner selves. We must face the problem of possible rejection and realize it is all right to show our true feelings and that it is all right to be rejected. Those who reject us are not worthy to be called our friends.

Those who truly love you will want to know the true you in any event. Have the courage to show the world who you really are and you may be in for a pleasant surprise.

● THE DEPRIVED TYPE

Some of us have a feeling of being fundamentally deprived. We feel the world owes us. This brings a feeling of emptiness that can never be filled and leaves us with a hunger for more. Deep inside ourselves we feel we will never be fulfilled. This can make us fiercely independent and afraid to ask for what we need because we fear it will not be given.

Sex is often used as a means of getting close and having contact, but if we are of this type then we feel that the partner will sense our detachment of feeling and lack of giving, and so will reject us.

Other people cannot fill the inner longing for recognition that is sought. Recognition of the true self can only come about when we show the world that we accept the fact that we are not the perfect, flawless human beings we wish to portray – when we stop living a lie.

Read the section on Covering Up (p. 11). It is very relevant.

● THE CONTROL TYPE

There are two main types who want to control and dominate others. One shouts and screams, bullies and overpowers others in order to get what he wants. However, he is no more dangerous than a dog that barks but does not bite.

It is the one who controls and dominates quietly and subtly, and who will manoeuvre everyone around him in order to achieve his ends, who is dangerous. Both are using other people as pawns in a game in which they need to win at all costs. Feelings and love are put aside, in this case, for it is only the conquest that really counts.

This type has no trust whatsoever in his fellow men. By being on top he avoids being vulnerable, but vulnerable he is and, contrary to appearances, sensitive in the extreme and often crying out for dependency.

He is so afraid of being controlled himself (being done to as he himself does) that he continues to control others to avoid becoming a victim himself and so having to face humiliation.

It comes down to asking himself why he is so much on the defensive. When he has answered that question, he will no longer feel the need to control others.

● THE SUBMISSIVE TYPE

There are those who grow up in a very rigid and often fiercely religious environment, crushed into a mould, dictated by unbending rules and regulations, where little demonstrative love is shown. The hardness of life is pointed out as part of daily existence.

This type has been taught not to show their feelings or emotions, for that would be seen as weakness. In this way, the show of emotions is held back by conditioning.

When adult, this type may be prone to violent rages and self-righteous anger, which seem to erupt for no apparent reason, but which stem from a desperate need for self-assertion. On the other hand, they may totally switch off and retire within their private world.

Outwardly, there is a show of tension. Underlying all actions is the fear that if they show emotion and feelings, they will be led again to submit to an outside control. This leads, in some cases, to a fierce independence.

Facing the realities of the background that has moulded their early life and finding forgiveness and understanding for those who, in the name of love, have moulded this type into submission, and learning that it is all right to show feeling and emotions will ultimately bring release and freedom to follow as their hearts dictate. This needs courage and conviction, both of which have to be fought for and acquired, step by step, without looking back.

● THE PRIDE TYPE

Fear of rejection by one or both parents experienced in early life will make this person seem outwardly aloof and totally in control, fiercely independent, never showing weakness to the outside world and rejecting others before they are themselves rejected. Their sensuality and character are used to get close to those they choose to have around them to provide comfort.

Behind the image of Pride they hide their desperate need of acceptance, which they seek in everything they do, though they would never admit to it. Recognition is of prime importance on all levels.

As a child, this pride type would perhaps have been beaten in order to subject their will to the adult and break their pride, but without success. This type will grow into a defiant adult seeking to prove himself to the world.

Their show of power and manipulation of the world around them is, with some pride types, very subtle. All is done to avoid being put on the spot or challenged. They protect themselves from too much probing and they appear very secretive in nature but can take ice-cold decisions without a second glance if it suits their purpose. Their inner self will avoid exposure by controlling their feelings and emotions.

Self-recognition is the key to change, to throwing off these barriers to further our growth. Without the will for self-examination and the desire to change ourselves, we can make no progress; we remain stuck in our types, experiencing only what that type allows and learning nothing new about ourselves or life.

- THE POSITIVE TYPE

> And once again the Prince of Peace has come,
> He is clothed in white, his sword is truth,
> His shield is faith, his belief innocence,
> His breath is love, his watchword peace.

> John-Andrew
> Patmos, Greece, 1978

This type demonstrates courage in the face of adversity which conquers fear. It is someone who is not afraid of responsibility or commitment,

*whose daily disciplines provide an anchor in the rough sea of life,

*who does not switch his allegiance, whatever the cost,

*whose nobility of soul never stoops to treachery even if his life or livelihood is at stake,

*whose word is his bond and whose vows are honoured,

*whose integrity is never questioned,

*whose inner strength and resourcefulness always prevail over life's obstacles,

*who shows anger only against those who break the code of decency,

*who is not afraid of his emotions,

*who shows confidence in hard work,

*who has no time for those who whisper in the night of treachery and plot against the light,

*who shows interest in all that comes towards him, however small,

*who puts his own needs last,

*who confronts grief with dignity of soul,

*who has the courage to live up to his ideals,

*who does not throw all caution to the wind as soon as he is attacked, but bides his time,

*who does not accept authority unless it tallies with his own perception of truth,
*who is not easily led but stands his ground,
*who knows no shame because his actions are true,
*who is not blinded by power or money,
*who will never betray a friend or his love whatever the reason,
*whose loyalty is first and foremost in his mind,
*who is gentle in his dealings with others but strong in his own convictions,
*who is never led but stands on his own ground,
*whose watchword is awareness less he fall into the traps set by those who follow darkness,
*whose goal is peace,
*whose actions are never excessive,
*who can sleep with a good conscience,
*who has purpose and never throws in his hand in adversity,
*who prizes truth and decency above all things,
*who cannot be beguiled by what the world of desire can offer.

The truth of what is presented here will best be proven by those who have already made part of this a reality in their lives. The will to become this type is in the grasp of a beggar or a prince; neither needs riches to achieve this nobility of soul.

At this stage, thoughts will no doubt come to mind which are in fact untrue. You may think, for example, that this type does not exist and that it is inaccessible, not human, and that there is no such person as this, that it is utopian. But now take a closer look and with a pencil tick the qualities that are already a part of you and you will be pleasantly surprised. If not then make it your goal to aspire to some of the qualities mentioned, to live with courage, dignity and self-respect. It is your right.

Look at history. There have been many who have left their footsteps in the sand and bequeathed an example to follow. Remember your childhood hero. Dig them out of your memory and start the process of changing your own personality, however uncomfortable that may be. It will bring with it joy and self-satisfaction in the long run. It will make you feel alive and help you towards a new beginning. While there is breath in your body it is never too late to start.

● COVERING UP

'To thine own self be true'

Some of you build a personality which you believe the world wants you to be, but which belies your real self.

What lengths do you go to, to perpetuate that deceit of the world and of yourself? What effort is required to keep up the pretence? It can eat up your very essence.

Again, choose, choose what is to be. Do you want to continue to live a lie? Or do you have the courage to show your weaknesses and face the possibility of rejection? Because after all, you built this edifice to be accepted by the world. What you face is non-acceptance of your real self. Have the courage to make up your mind, cease this pretence and be true to yourself.

What a relief this will be. It will bring the possibility of a new beginning where you can live with yourself. After all, look at those whom you have tried to impress, were they worthy of all your efforts?

Redirect your energies to a worthwhile pursuit and leave the artificial you behind for ever. You will find there is no more insecurity. No more fear of being found out.

If you live a lie, what is the next step? Imagine it.

Emotions

While it is through the physical senses that we experience the world, it is largely through our emotions that we interpret it and our relationship to it. The emotions give warmth and feeling, but through them factual perception and logic are all too easily ruled by imagination. Reason gives way to sentiment.

If logic and reason can interpret the information sent in by the senses and produce a conclusion that would change as the information changes, it is emotion that clouds our vision and leads to a state in which we do not see things as they are.

In the Game of Life not seeing things as they are is like not seeing the ball clearly when playing tennis, or not knowing where the white lines are. The player needs to understand his emotions, what he is, how he functions and how to prevent himself from taking a negative role. For it is that negative role that hampers his performance and holds him back in his development.

That emotions have both a positive and a negative role is an idea that few would dispute. To be without emotion is to be unfeeling, to have no contact with the human condition. But all people have experience of negative emotions such as fear and anger. We talk freely about emotions but do not really stop to think what they are. Without having that understanding of what emotions are and what they are doing to us we cannot analyse the way in which emotions disturb our balance and what that should teach us about ourselves and our relationship with the world.

We begin by looking at the negative emotions.

● APATHY – THE DEFEATED

Apathy is a state of mind in which we have given up and no longer exercise control over our lives. It is included in this discussion of emotions as it represents the lowest state of emotional energy, as well as physical and mental energy.

Apathy occurs as a result of our suppressing negative emotions and feelings, not being able or prepared to deal with them and so letting them accumulate in our unconscious mind. As we do this we are less and less able to act positively as we resort to distractions and procrastination to prevent us dealing with what we have suppressed and keep our minds as quiet as possible. When we have allowed this state to dominate us we are in the state of apathy.

At this point, where we have little or no capacity left to discriminate, we become almost unable to feel anything, whether good or bad. In our deadened state of apathy, we become very negative. 'Why bother?' and 'who cares?' are phrases that are typical of this lack of energy.

Apathy is a state of mind. It is the state of being in a rut, just carrying on with something without clear decisions or purpose. Some of us spend all our lives in this dreamy, inert state. We go to work, eat, sleep, get married, have children, get divorced, always just going through the motions without being involved, without sparkle, without real enjoyment or genuine pain. Those of us who are apathetic are usually tired, cynical and very draining to be with, because we drag others down to our level, or try to.

This is the 'I cannot', the 'I've given up' state with absence of feelings, energy, vitality, enthusiasm, sometimes to the point where we may never try again. Apathy is an extreme feeling that we no longer have control over our lives or the things that sweep us along. It makes us play dead. We just give up and go through the motions and we let our negativity harden inside us.

We put things off until we feel more like doing them, until we have more energy. However, doing them would make us feel better and re-energize us! It would relieve us of the burden of suppressed emotion.

Action

Action overcomes apathy. This is simple but true. If you can understand what your apathy is about you will realize that the only way to overcome it is to act. Even if you have to force yourself you must pick yourself up and do something. You will start to feel better.

Go for a walk. Fresh air and exercise begin the process.

Tidy your house or your office. This will always make you feel more able and ready to tackle anything.

Take up a new interest or hobby. The enthusiasm you feel will rub off on the rest of your life.

Whatever you do, you need to let fresh air clear away the staleness of apathy and only action will do that.

- ANGER — THE DESTROYER

Anger is a reaction to other people and to ourselves that stems from two cycles:

Frustration –   towards others
                who take it out on us
                who continue the cycle

Intolerance –   towards others
                who take it out on us
                who continue the cycle

Fear of anger

There is a paradox that we are often afraid of our own anger. It is quite understandable to be afraid of the anger of others who make life unpleasant for us, but few of us have the courage and conviction to face the process of anger.

We can still be afraid of expressing our anger, unable to vent our rage. It is as though we cannot reach an expression that is midway between total holding in and violent, destructive rage. We have to learn to communicate and that means conquering our fear of that process.

There can be many reasons for our anger:

Frustration at work –   anger towards the job
                        anger towards the people we work with
                        anger at ourselves for taking the job
                        anger at ourselves for not making more of ourselves

What to do?

If the job is frustrating, change to something else. If we work with people who anger us, why take it on board?

Are we angry with ourselves and blaming something or someone else? This is often the case. We have to learn tolerance, to look at our behaviour and to stop being self-righteous. If someone else is annoying us either deliberately or unconsciously, then we have to talk to them to explain the effect they are having on us. We must learn to sort it out, to be open and to express ourselves. Not doing so only damages us.

If we do not face our anger or frustration at work, we take it home with us and because we feel safer and more secure with those at home, we direct our anger and frustration at them. How many of us can say that someone changed when they took on a certain job or changed when something happened at work. They say 'I'm all right' or 'I'm fine' when we know, as a friend or a partner, that there is something wrong but the opportunity to share the problem is not taken. Instead they become angry when asked about it because they are not all right and are not coping. It is often guilt or fear that stops us from telling the truth.

A man will frequently fall into this trap because he 'must not' show weakness and 'must' be seen to be doing everything well. What frail vanity we have! At home our relationships are far more strained by not expressing our feelings than by the silent death of suppressing them. We become inwardly angry because our partner fails to live up to our expectations, instead of offering them the opportunity to discuss things with tolerance and understanding. An obsessively tidy person will demand the same standards of their partner, without caring that the other may have different priorities, or just not share their obsession. This can lead to mutual anger and resentment and to a partner feeling worthless and depressed.

There are so many ways in which our intolerance will trigger an angry response either in ourselves or others. It is a lack of respect, a feeling of our own superiority and our pride that lie at the root of this response. We feel we are better than others and that they should come up to our standards.

If someone at work is not pulling their weight, we must be straightforward and talk to them without anger, remaining tolerant even if they are cynical. We cannot wait until our anger and frustration injures us and our families and loved ones. High blood-pressure, headaches and tension are the end result of keeping anger bottled up.

We must be tolerant of others who do not have our gifts or drive as each of us can only perform to the extent of our own personal capacity. Try to understand this.

We are often frustrated by our children and angry with them. It may be that we need to offer love, support and encouragement rather than using anger to force a child into what we believe they should or should not do. All of us should feel special and that we matter. We should feel that what we do has value, whatever it is.

If we see something in others that makes us angry, if they are causing hurt or pain, then our first task is to look at ourselves. Often the thing about others that makes us angry is a fault we have in ourselves. We have to look for it.

If we can truly say we are free of that fault and our understanding is such that our motives do not stem from intolerance, *then* we can be angry. We can speak our minds then and there – being honest but not destructive. We must be prepared to learn from the experience, however. We may be wrong sometimes but we should not be afraid of this. We must be prepared to learn to improve.

We have to do this as to suppress anger is to turn our negativity inward. Some people do this to such an extent that although they never get angry, they are not always kind or tolerant, and can be cold, dogmatic people. These people are afraid of anger to such an extent that they are dishonest.

This is an area in which the term 'stress' should be more clearly understood. The results are often appalling if we are not able to unload stress as we receive it by letting our feelings out. Spitefulness, mental cruelty and crimes of violence are all to do with negative emotions spilling over. Often, those who reach such a pitch have not been taught to deal with negative emotions.

We have all had these emotions but when they reach such a pitch that our suppression of them cannot cope, we explode, turning against whoever or whatever is in our way in an attempt to destroy it. These destructive feelings are the ones that we have to learn to shed.

To recognize that we have these feelings is important. This is often the big one, the big step, to be able to look in the mirror and say 'I am angry'.

Solutions

Write down what you are angry about and then examine what is written. Work out the real priorities. Decide to change. Recognize anger and see how destructive it is to you and to others around you, including those who love you and whom you love. Then you will want to do something about it.

Divert anger into some activity where it will not hurt others: a walk or a run after work when you first get home will often blow away most of the daily stress.

Take a cold shower – but more of that later.

Take up sport if you want to compete without hurting others. Many sports are a form of disciplined warfare.

Learn to communicate at the 'niggle' stage, before anger builds up.

Ask for help.

● DESIRE – THE TRAP

We live, act, move, are temporarily satisfied, enjoy and suffer principally for the satisfaction of desire. Desire, it is said, is one of the prime motivating powers of human existence and we believe that to curtail desire would be to leave life without meaning. However, desire is often not only linked with our emotions but also distorted by them. We tend to pursue goals that weaken our will and clog up our view.

Being deprived of the goals, our desire eats us up and leaves us dissatisfied and with a sense of longing. At the root of desire is the longing to take that which we feel we lack. It is our need for possession and instant gratification which we pursue with such intensity, whatever the costs. Desire brings in its wake sorrow, unrest and disappointment.

The pursuit of desire brings with it intense excitement and satisfaction when it is reached. Yet, when we finally gain the object of our desire, we are baffled by the constant emptiness we still feel. The irony is that having frittered our energies away in our endeavour to possess the object of our desire, having done all we can, even lied or deceived in order to obtain the object of our desire, we lose interest in that object because, whether consciously or not, we realize that we have not found lasting satisfaction or peace of mind. We do not understand that we have become the slaves of our desire and have created a net around ourselves, by our thoughts and actions. We feel empty, and we are then driven by this emptiness.

In the end, it should not be our desire but rather the consciously felt will of our true nature, free of emotional entanglement, that remains as the sole initiator of our action. We are under the illusion that motivation ends without desire, but this is not so. When we are ruled and guided from within, and not governed by impulse and emotions, we are still fulfilling our desire but are not *ruled* by it.

Our desire can be for physical satisfaction, for wealth, power or the need for recognition, for satisfying the intellect or our heart, or simply for the seeking of plea-sure. We can even be drawn into the need to fulfil our ideals, put forward our political ambitions, as well as the desire to see our religious beliefs accepted by others. However, when we are prepared to be guided from within, it is no longer emotional desire that drives us, but the purity and clarity of reason, dictated by the 'pure will' of our hearts.

Gautama Buddha looked on himself as a doctor and discovered the correct diagnosis of man's suffering. He then proposed a cure. He showed that nothing is per-manent, even our joys, because all things pass and we know it. As a dew drop on a rose disappears in the heat of the sun, so everything in our life eventually passes. Buddha said that our desire is not in our circum-stances, but is within ourselves and our attitude to our circumstances. Therefore, if we change our attitude, we get rid of the craving that produces suffering.

Buddha was nothing if not thorough. He described eight principles to adhere to in order to free ourselves from suffering:

1. Having the right understanding: recognizing how our suffering comes about.
2. Having the right attitude: unselfishness and compassion.
3. Watching what we say: which includes silence when we have nothing to say.
4. Following right action: acting only from our true feelings, not governed by the distortions of emotion, also taking care of our bodies and not polluting them or our minds – read the section on Listening Within (pp. 58–64).
5. Having the right livelihood: doing the kind of job where right action can be practised without compromise.
6. Making the right effort: accepting the need to pursue moral, mental and spiritual disciplines without losing heart.
7. Right recollection: developing our awareness and concentration until our unruly nature is firmly under control.
8. Right meditation: the true meaning of meditation is a training of the mind to its limits until we have reached a point where we are fully aware of our true nature and free from our desires, fears and intolerance.

For a moment draw yourself back from your desires. Try an exercise. Sit down with a pen and paper and make a list of the things you have wanted to do in the past few years. Include also those items which you wanted to have in the past but dismissed because you thought you could not have them or simply forgot about them.

Decide now what you really wanted to do, and what, with hindsight, would have been good for you to do or have. Try to reflect on the consequences, both for yourself and for others, of having taken each course of action.

- PRIDE –THE STUCK EGO

Pride is a state in which people seek attention and recognition for what they think they are and what they think they have done.

Pride causes us to want to be seen as the best, but we will often use the strategy of holding others back to make sure we stay there. Pride is occupied with sitting on your laurels and telling others about it. It can even make us cutting and unpleasant in our personalities, as a way of putting others down.

Pride is often a fear of not being able to sustain a success. Unconsciously we feel it was a fluke and we are afraid of being found out. As a defence mechanism, we put on a show of superiority to keep people intimidated so that no one will think we are vulnerable.

Pride holds onto the past and so prevents us from moving forward and achieving more with our lives. This will stay in our nature until we become aware of the process and let go of the chains that pride puts around us.

We may overcome our individual pride but if pride is in our nature, then it will colour all our thoughts and actions. This does not mean we have to put ourselves down all the time: this would just be false humility, which is another subtle form of pride.

We must understand that there are two forms of pride. Pride in our accomplishments is constructive and helpful, as long as we do not become stuck in the acclaim or the desire for it. Pride of this nature helps to maintain good standards. But negative pride keeps us in a state of mind that resists change. That prevents us from being receptive to life and therefore also from receiving its benefits.

To begin to remedy this emotional block, start to notice when you are looking for praise or recognition, and in doing so, start talking about or bringing to someone else's notice something you have not done so well. Puncture that balloon!

To deflate the ego that pride feeds, begin to write down your positive and negative qualities. You do not need anyone to do this for you. Do not be afraid – have a clear look. Then a little genuine humility will help you to work on the negative side and this will get you going on the right track.

We must learn to notice pride that is stuck in others because this will help us to recognize it in ourselves. Do not worry that you are being judgemental – we do not want to be judged for the pride we see in ourselves.

We must also learn from criticism, and learn not to put our pride in the way like a brick wall if we are criticized. Look at the criticism for any opportunity to learn from it and to change, without wallowing in self-pity. Pride cannot co-exist with reprogramming, reconditioning and the breaking of habits if these are done with a wish to improve ourselves.

Recognize also the achievements of others. If we can get out from behind pride, we can begin to see with genuine appreciation the efforts and accomplishments of other people.

This is hard for proud people. We have to feel no

one else is as good as us and we usually put others down to make ourselves seem on top, even if we try to make positive comments such as 'Your garden is looking nice. It was always so untidy.' Or 'You look well. It's great to see you not looking as drawn and haggard as usual.'

Get out of this habit of making digs about people. Learn to look for what is positive in others and not for what is negative. Teach yourself.

● JEALOUSY – THE GREEN-EYED MONSTER

Discontent, hatred, anger, doubt, inferiority complexes, suspicion, mistrust, envy, resentment, bitterness, animosity, vindictiveness, spite, irritation, annoyance, indignation, malice, prejudice – these are all part of the green-eyed monster called jealousy. Jealousy is not a comfortable bedfellow and if not restrained can devour its creator.

Often jealousy comes from making judgements based on assertions that we believe to be true but belie the reality of the situation. Thus we act on assumptions based on insufficient evidence – consider the action and outcome of jealousy that is portrayed in Shakespeare's *Othello*.

Yes, jealousy is futile, but so often we cannot rid ourselves of its components and reason ourselves back to a state of equilibrium. This is when it is good to sit down with pen and paper and analyse why we are jealous. So often we have fallen into the trap of jealousy because we have judged other people, or even ourselves or our situation. This will only bring about grief for what do we really know about ourselves or someone else? We do not have enough evidence to judge. Maybe not having what we crave for is exactly what we need for our development or to give us time and the space to reflect on what we truly want! Read the section on Free Will (pp. 84–86).

The turmoil brought about by our wants can make us very vulnerable and afraid. Read the section on Fear (pp. 26–30).

Acknowledge your jealousy, laugh at your unreasonable behaviour, and don't take yourself so seriously. Try to see a given situation as it truly is when not enhanced by the torture inflicted by your imagination. Don't lose your balance and have a tantrum but face the situation and see if you really want to be drawn into it.

Jealousy is often brought about by a feeling of lack: lack of love; lack of understanding from others; lack of career advancement; lack of money; lack of opportunity – we could go on indefinitely.

Jealousy is also linked with the question *why*? and what we feel we are owed. Why should I have to live in a one-bedroom flat when others have spacious houses? Why should I stand by and see others have someone to love when I have no one? Why must I struggle constantly against the odds when others find it so easy? Why are others handed over opportunities on a plate when I have to fight for them?

You have two choices: one is to indulge in jealousy, the other is to make a statement to yourself:

To hold your head up high.
To feel joy when you are surrounded by disaster.
To have hope when everything seems hopeless.
To give when everything is taken from you.
To commit yourself when everyone has let you down.
To love when you have been betrayed in love all your life.

To trust when your trust in others has been shattered.
To take responsibility for others when all you know is the opposite.
To be just when you have not received justice.
To give hope when you have none yourself.
To give joy when all you have received is rebuke.
To create beauty out of ugliness.
To be honourable towards others when none have treated you with honour.
To give of yourself when you have no strength to give.
To be able to stand and say 'I have done my best, I can do no more' allows you to have self-respect, and that is something no one can take away!

You should ask yourself whether you make the best of what you have, however little.

● FEAR – THE LITTLE DEATH

If there has been an oppressor that has held the human spirit in chains, then it is fear itself.

The way in which fear can control people's minds and actions is a process as old as human experience. It has been exploited to a degree by all human beings to hurt and control each other, and has affected the lives of everyone that has ever lived.

Yet we stop short of analysing what it is. We fail to know its strengths and weaknesses and the way in which we can choose whether to have fear in our lives, or not.

Often we are not even aware that fear is affecting our lives because we are so conditioned to living with it. We have to become acquainted with the manifestations of fear before we can break its grip. These manifestations can take many forms:

Fear of failure – often this is why people procrastinate.
Fear of losing one's job.
Fear of being criticized.
Fear of being alone.
Fear of being unable to cope with existing problems.
Fear of losing control of one's emotions.
Fear of losing control over others.
Fear of letting go.
Fear of losing what we never had in the first place.
Fear of being found out.
Fear of the truth and what it makes us do.
Fear of not being accepted.
Fear of not belonging.

There are so many forms of fear. We can even be afraid of fear itself or the chaos it brings to our inner world. It is fear that stops us from living a life of fulfilment.

It is essential to recognize how fear comes about and how to cope with it. First and foremost, we have to understand that we rarely fear what we have found to be true. Rather, we fear what has not previously been within the realms of our experience: the unknown, or what could be. It is the information with which we feed our computer, our unconscious programming and our negative reactions to these images – or even our imaginations being used negatively – which all fuel fear.

For instance, if a rumour circulates in the office that there will be redundancies, how many of those who hear this will feel fear: 'it may be me who loses my job . . . '? Exactly. That rumour will trigger our store of images about loss of status, loss of income, threats to home, security and so on. These images were in our unconscious already. All we had to experience was the trigger and off we went into a state of fear. The more we accept this fear, the more we produce the images to support its reality. Few will react by thinking that their redundancy was just what they needed – even if this is, in fact, true.

In other words, we are our own worst enemy. By taking a particular line of thought, we bring out of our memory banks the shadows of past events that form an analogy with our present fear. It is these negative imaginings which make the fear an even greater reality. Fear can be thought of as a force in itself which we feed – the more we feed our fears, the stronger the force becomes and the more it assails us. Do not wrestle with your fears, because that is how the force behind the fear increases. We have to realize that fear cannot exist without us. If we do not give fear our energy, our imagination, our life blood, it dies because it has no hold over us.

In an extreme example, imagine you have been told you have an incurable disease. Your whole world is instantly changed. Why? Because someone told you something and your imagination got to work, generating negative thoughts and images that gripped you. Both your internal and external world changed because someone spoke a few words.

In the instance of disease, we must consider whether the doctors have made a mistake. Is there a cure that they do not know about? Will we be the people who will have the task and experience of finding this cure? Ask yourself, 'Do I have to lie down and die, because someone said so? Just what is it that I am afraid of? Is it pain, or death?' The reality is always worse if it is clouded with fear.

Our world can also become black with fear of the

future. We might surrender to fear, which is when it will eat us completely, leaving us paralysed and unable to act or think clearly. This is the time to know how fear works and to tackle it in the right way. Instead of feeding our fear, we must start to detach ourselves from it.

We must begin by analysing it and using our powers of reason to bring the 'light of understanding' to the dark hole that fear makes its own, with our permission. The shadows of a mouse projected upon the wall in such a way could make us believe a monster lurked around the corner. However, by confronting our fear and shedding light upon the monster, we would see what was really there: a mouse. We must look at the fear with our eyes and heart, and begin to bring calm to the storm of our emotions.

Ask yourself, 'Am I responding to someone else's fear?' For example, a large part of exam nerves are due to students promoting fear in each other and then 'picking up' that atmosphere.

We must recognize that many unexpected things can happen in our lives and accept that we cannot live without taking risks. In order to overcome fear, we have to begin to ask ourselves, 'What am I afraid of?'

Take control by writing down your fears. Do not automatically expect the worst, as that is negative programming – a negative habit. What we are doing, if we expect a negative outcome, is providing our fear with food from the imagination. If a negative thought is about to enter your mind try to become aware of it before it has had time to take root in your unconscious and put it aside, replacing it with a positive thought.

It is important to understand that we are breaking a

habit, for we have been conditioned to react in this way. Just consider the idea that fear is a hungry creature that wants to feed off our energy and see how easily it has trained us to provide that nourishment at the push of an idea. Like one of Pavlov's dogs, we give obediently. It takes time to react differently.

Speak to yourself, convince yourself of the positive reality. The more we practise, the less we will be plagued with fear. Be patient and stick with it.

There are some people who attract fear, who gather things to worry about, to frighten themselves and to avoid behaving differently. We do not have to – that is our choice. Others have the courage to tackle their fears, perhaps remembering the phrase 'Feel the fear and do it anyway'.

In Frank Herbert's novel *Dune*, there is a litany which is part of some of the character training. It is worth relating:

I must not fear.
Fear is the mind killer.
Fear is the little death that brings total obliteration.
I will face my fear.
I will permit it to pass over me and through me.
When it has gone past, I will turn my inner eye to see its path.
And when the fear has gone there will be nothing. Only I will remain.

After facing your fear you will be stronger by knowing yourself more deeply and fear will no longer be sapping your vital energy. In order to become acquainted with our fears, we need to recognize some of the key outlooks and actions which we associate with fear. Make a list of what triggers your own fear. Become aware of

the subtlety of your fear and then reprogramme yourself.

● HOW DOES NEGATIVITY MANIFEST ITSELF?

Let us look, first of all, at the two sides of our brain.
The left side is a highly sophisticated computer which,
under deep hypnosis, would give you the data regis-
tered five years ago recording the number, make and
colour of the car which was standing outside your home
at the time. The left side has all the data of every
experience you have ever had – good, bad and indiffer-
ent – since the time you were in your mother's womb.
There is a great deal of written evidence available on
the subject for those who care to take a deeper look.

So, for a moment, consider a long-distance runner
who has collapsed near to the finish on one occasion.
In subsequent races this will be on their mind and create
a major obstacle to future success. 'Will I fail again?'
What has brought this about at this point in the race is
not the result of his lack of effort, but the computer
which is the left-hand side of the brain, projecting
against the inner screen of his mind, all his failures in
past events. This projection has given data, evidence
and instances of these failures and the runner's collapse
is his reaction to the outpouring of this data. Of course,
there could be other reasons.

This is precisely how negativity works. It uses the left
side of our brain to project past failures, thus actively
interfering with our ability to overcome the negative
impact that we face.

There are visualization techniques practised in sports
that we can use to reprogramme the left part of the
brain (more information on these and other visualization techniques can be found on pp. 70–79). Firstly,

deep relaxation is used, then a tape is played giving new instructions and overriding the data currently present in the left side of the brain. The tape could say, using the runner's own voice: 'This time, when I arrive at 500 metres before the end, new vigour and strength will enter into my being. I will have enough breath and stamina to reach my goal.'

Again, this method is well-documented for those who wish to read about it.

What is interesting, is that the outer negative force seeks within the data of your left brain, the evidence of your failure on a given subject. This tangible negative force then activates the left side of your brain and projects onto the inner screen of your mind the failures mentioned earlier. This destroys your impetus and your courage to confront your fears. With loss of hope, you do not want to try again.

This plays totally into the hands of the negative forces. If you give in to the fears which are projected onto the inner screen of your mind, you make your intentions to overcome them impossible and you will be weighed down by your past failures, finding you lack the courage to confront the problem or the person who in the past has won over you. Thus you play into the hands of that force which desires your downfall and wishes to hinder your inner progress, leaving you to shut the gate on the prison you have built for yourself, afraid to step out and to try anew to overcome your weaknesses.

There is a purpose in the negative force's attempt to use you as a pawn. Negativity cannot exist without your giving it life. Negativity is unmanifested matter. Your fear is its life blood. Darkness needs light to become manifest. It looks to you to provide it with that light. This is why it has to set the stage by exploiting your reactions and using your fear. You provide the food that negativity needs to exist, for without your fear, it cannot exist.

How, you may ask, can you cease being a pawn?

Firstly, as you perceive your old fears welling up within you, as you try to tackle the same old problem and are paralysed by the thought of failure, look at the screen of your mind. Stand back, look at the data and, in your mind, take a cloth and wipe the screen clear of your past failures. Give thanks within yourself for the lessons of your life that have allowed you to gain these experiences. Be proud of the scars that are left on your soul, for these are part of your humanity and can be worn with honour.

Stand up and make a positive statement. As long as you identify with the negative messages that trick you into becoming a victim to negativity, then you will be used. So, start to make new statements:

'I am worthy to be loved.'
'I can make it and overcome.'

PART TWO

_Your Body
The Precious Vessel_

Exercise

- WHY DO IT?

Our lives are constantly in motion; changes occur every day to which we must adapt. To do so requires a flexible mind and a strong will, but to carry the mind and the will requires a strong and fluid body.

As with all things in life, we must move towards balance and harmony of the body. The health benefits and disciplines gained enhance the balance between our mind and body and make us more able to achieve our aims and to counter disease. If we cultivate our intellect and not our bodies, we are out of balance and ill health will result. If we cultivate our bodies but not our minds, we are also out of balance.

Exercise is using your body in a way that will promote health. Yet, as with diet, emotions, mental attitudes and spiritual values, the subject of exercise is full of prejudice and misconceptions. Many people do not like to exercise. There are a variety of reasons for this, which may be deeply rooted in our past. For instance:

1. Being mocked at school for not having any skill at games.
2. Being overweight, when young or in your adult life.
3. Being too ill or debilitated to take any exercise.
4. Not liking sports.

The counters to these are:

1. Remember it is now your life. If you let the past dictate the present and prejudice your quality of life, then you may be the loser. Look at the section on Fear (pp. 26–30). Consider how you face the fear of what others think of you. Decide to act.
2. As you make the choice to become in control of your own life, you also take control of your body. Exercise, gently at first, and let it be a part of your programme of change.
3. Fear of failure should not deter you from trying. See how much better you feel.
4. Gentle exercise such as walking is as valid when you are old as it is when you are young. In China huge numbers of elderly people practise Tai Chi and it is a joy to watch the grace and beauty of old age still fluid and in motion.

There is a law in physics, identified by Isaac Newton, which says in essence that everything falls apart without energy: if you do not maintain your house, it will fall down; if you do not look after your business, it will fall apart. It is the same with the body.

Even if we eat and drink well, we become sluggish inside without exercise to stimulate the metabolism. If our energy is not used, then our body's ability to provide energy is also lost. Stagnation of the functions of the body is identified as a medical condition in China, and is a state that will lead to illness.

● SPORT

Sport is exercise that satisfies more than just the physical needs of our body; it is exercise that aims to fulfil other sets of needs and drives.

However, violent sports that make excessive demands on the body with little preparation, can do more harm than good. Squash is one of these: there is nothing wrong with the game, but very few people warm up well before playing, and so they make a sudden demand on the body which imposes stress on the heart.

Sport that invokes excessive emotion, especially anger and aggression, may not suit our need for balance and peace of mind, and this can be destructive to our striving for harmony.

However, there are those who need to learn to become assertive and come out of themselves, or to overcome their fears. Sports such as judo or fencing can provide for these needs beyond fitness.

As with all things in life, consider why you are making a choice. If the choice is made in response to your inner feelings, your gut feelings, then go with it. You are listening to your needs and fulfilling them.

● STRESS STAGNATION

Don't choose aggressive, adrenaline-inducing activities but use exercise to activate the body fully as our nervous system and chemistry have primed our bodies for this purpose.

Exercise on this level will calm the mind, improve digestion and increase the metabolic rate of the body, enabling us to detoxify and provide the vitality that only comes with balance.

● HOW MUCH?

Regular light exercise is safer and more effective than occasional bouts of strenuous exercise.

A walk before breakfast every day or exercise done after work every day – say a fifteen-minute run, a game of tennis or another walk – is very much better for you than a game of rugby once a week and nothing else.

● WHAT EXERCISE?

Walking briskly, not sluggishly, in fresh air is still the best all-round exercise.

Morning is the best time. Get out of bed, have a cold shower and walk before breakfast every day – the earlier the better. The less you feel like it, the more you need it. Walking clears the mind and removes stale air from the lungs. When done briskly it will warm you up, activating your metabolism, eliminating stress-induced chemicals from the body, and exercising muscles and joints. Take a walk every day for a month, at the same time every day and feel the results.

There are many other forms of exercise. Gardening is good, but as our backs so readily tell us, large infrequent doses can hurt. Cycling is excellent and takes our body weight off the feet.

Oriental disciplines of exercise such as Tai Chi Chuan and Qi Gung may sound strange and difficult, but are probably the most rewarding forms of exercise in terms of health. These can be simple to learn, but take a lifetime to master fully.

Running suits some people but not others. Much of the benefit of running can be lost if we do not know how to run. Often we try to run too fast and land on our heels with consequent shock to our knees and the rest of our bodies. You may have seen a film of the African tribe, the Masai, running: they run on their toes. If you begin by running on your toes very slowly, even at walking pace, you will be able to obtain the benefits without strain. And only go faster when you feel you can. Listen to your body and see what you are comfortable with.

● BREATHING

You will have become aware at times of the way in which you breathe. Breathing is not a function that is detached from your emotional and mental states – just the opposite, in fact, the way you breathe reflects the state you are in.

When you are asleep your breathing becomes deep, slow and forceful. When you are under strain your breathing becomes shallow and rapid. When you are angry your breathing can be quite irregular. Yet when you are relaxed your breathing is slow, rhythmic and quiet. Just as our state alters our breathing, we can consciously change our state by altering our breathing.

With a knowledge of breathing exercises you can control a state of panic or distress, steady yourself, reduce tension, lower blood pressure and even cholesterol levels. Breathing techniques can be used both for 'First Aid' and to prevent stress and tension from injuring your body.

Regular breathing exercises, especially done early in the morning when the air is fresh, will clear the mind and invigorate the body. You may have dismissed the Japanese exercising before work or the Chinese performing their Tai Chi routines, but when you have undertaken a few exercise disciplines yourself you will admire their dedication.

The following exercises are drawn from the Chinese knowledge of breathing and exercise. The terms in which they are described have been adapted to make them more accessible to the Western reader.

First Aid

'First Aid' breathing exercises are those you can use when you find you are under stress. It might be that you are having a hectic day at work and you feel that things are getting to you, or you might be stuck in a traffic jam with your pulse racing and the frustration making you angry. Learn to recognize the signs and anticipate situations that will make you tense, anxious or uptight.

This simple breathing exercise is the most important for 'First Aid'. It is an exercise to bring about a state of calm.

1. Sit comfortably in a chair consciously letting your shoulders drop and move outward to widen the chest.
2. Let your head float upwards from your shoulders as if it was being lifted from above.
3. Look straight ahead as if gazing at a place on a wall. Practise this initial letting go. Don't force it, be comfortable. It may take time for you to get the knack. Don't feel defeated: it's just something new you needed to learn.

When you can do this easily your lungs will be free to fill from top to bottom, so take a few deep, slow but gentle breaths. You are now ready to start the calming breathing.

Breathe in freely to the count of three and out again also to the count of three. Let the chest expand and deflate as you breathe. Try not to exaggerate the movements.

This is a way of controlling your stress response, quietening the nervous system and getting yourself back in balance.

Once you have got the knack of this you can do it anywhere, whenever you need it. It is so simple and yet so effective.

Breathing exercise to help you sleep

This is to help people whose minds won't switch off from the events of the day.

Go to bed and make yourself ready for sleep. Close your eyes and make yourself comfortable. Breathe deeply and gently, letting the stomach expand and contract, deepening the breathing.

Try to visualize your breath as you exhale moving up from the diaphragm, through the lungs and out of the mouth. In your mind's eye, watch the air follow an arc like a rainbow from your mouth, back to your stomach and through an imaginary hole back to the diaphragm. Then start again with a slow rhythm, breathing and seeing the breath flow through the lungs and over its arc back to the diaphragm. Breathe in from the diaphragm slowly through the chest to the mouth counting 1–2–3–4 then blow it back to the diaphragm with another 1–2–3–4. Keep visualizing the circle of air as it moves through you and round to the diaphragm. Keep your mind fully involved with this process and you will find sleep gently enfolds you.

Tension reducing

When you feel strain and tension in your neck and shoulders, there is a simple exercise that can reduce the stiffness and pain. You can do it at home or at work just when you feel you need it. You may find that you need to do this exercise several times a day when you're under pressure or feel tense. That's all right – it is better to disperse the feeling than to let it build up.

Stand up, stretch your arms above your head, then let them fall loosely to your sides. Straighten your back, hold in your stomach, tuck your bottom under you, let your head rise and your shoulders drop. This will encourage the blood to flow.

Take a slow in-breath counting 1–2–3–4. Hold it in 1–2–3–4 then breathe out 1–2–3–4. At the same time allow your shoulders to drop further. Now make a circle with your head, let it drop onto your chest, roll the head over the left shoulder, let it drop behind you and roll over the right shoulder and back onto the chest. Roll the head three times to the left, then three times to the right, breathing easily all the time. Finally lift the head, take a deep steady breath and you will feel less tired and tense.

Regular breathing exercises

To be done every morning out of doors in the fresh air.

Refreshing Breathing – to clear feelings of stagnation.
Stand with your feet shoulder-width apart. Take a deep in-breath through your nose. As you do so, come up onto your toes, hands and fingers out-stretched above your head, then in one quick puff let out all the breath through your mouth. At the same time come off your

toes, bend at the waist so you end up bent forward with your hands almost touching the ground. Do this exercise three times.

Balancing Breathing – do this more often when you have colds or sore throats.
Stand with feet shoulder-width apart. Breathe in through your nose and out through your mouth. Clench your fists and bring them up to shoulder height, knuckles upward, elbows at your sides. Open your fists and as you breathe out, slowly through your mouth, push your palms forward, fingers upwards. Time it so the breath runs out as the arms reach full stretch, then breathe in through your nose and at the same time, start to clench your fists and bend your elbows so that they are again near your shoulders, elbows down. Repeat this exercise six times. Finally, on an in-breath, let the hands come in and then as you breathe out, let the arms float down to your sides. This exercise is very good for sore throats.

Energizing Breathing – to invigorate.
Stand with your feet just over shoulder-width apart. Bend your knees slightly. Breathe in through your nose and at the same time bring your hands to shoulder height, palms facing forward. Breathe out through your mouth slowly. At the same time, push the palms and arms forward. Imagine you are pushing against a heavy weight. Breathe in through your nose and draw the hands back to the shoulders.

Now as you breathe out again through your mouth, push the palms to the sides at shoulder height. Imagine you are parting two walls. Again as you breathe out, push the palms above your head then breathe in once more. Bring the palms back to shoulder height, turn the palms to face down and then, as you breathe out, push the palms down and then let them rest at your sides. Take three breaths and then repeat the Energizing Breathing so that you do it three times altogether.

Exercises for our internal organs

We are used to the idea of exercises for our muscular body and even breathing exercises but the following are for our major internal organs. These help the functions of our organs aiding elimination, digestion and invigorating internal function.

For the Stomach – to charge the organs and aid the digestion.
Standing with your feet together, place your left hand on your stomach. Bring your right hand to shoulder height, with your elbow and arm to your right side, your palm facing in front of you. Breathe in through your nose. Now breathe out slowly through your mouth. At the same time push your right palm out in front of you. Time the outward motion with your outward breath. Then breathe in through your nose and draw in your right hand back to its starting position. Do this exercise three times and then increasing over a period of three weeks to six times. When you have finished this move, place your right hand on your stomach and the left hand on top of your right hand. Do three in and out breaths.

The Liver
Standing with heels together, breathe in through your nose and come up on your toes at the same time. Turn your head to the right as you breathe out slowly through your mouth. Lower your heels and turn your

head to face forward. Repeat, but turn your head to the left. Do this exercise three times to each side and increase after practice.

The Kidneys
Stand with your feet just over shoulder-width apart, knees bent. Place your palms together in front of you, fingers pointing in opposite directions. Hold the hands level with the abdomen approximately 9 inches in front of you. Now reverse the position by rotating the hands but keeping them touching. Keep going through this motion twenty-one times. Each time you change, turn just your head to look to the side, first the right then the left. Press hard on the palms, as this creates heat which you can direct. When you have finished, place your right hand on your right kidney and your left hand on your left kidney. Hold this position for at least a minute. You will feel the warmth flow from your hands. Relax for a minute or so.

The 'S' Breath
This is a special exercise for the lungs. It also provides relief for colds and helps to unblock energy.

Lie on your back, arms by your side, legs lying loosely out straight. Take a long in-breath through your nose. As you do so, take your arms up and then down to rest on the floor above your head. Now make a very loud *esss* sound and continue the sound slowly until you run out of breath. At the same time let your hands lift up in a semi-circular motion and come down to your sides. Repeat three times.

Rest and Relaxation

The object of rest and relaxation is to enable our bodies to recover balance, to detoxify and to regenerate. It is also an opportunity for psychological regeneration – this is accepted wisdom.

However, this is the product of a largely passive approach to rest and relaxation, seeing such time as a non-activity to recover from activity. If rest and relaxation are approached with the same openness and with the same willingness to learn as the changing of negative emotional states and our health, they can be used to heal us and to strengthen our health and emerging state of mind.

If rest and relaxation are purely passive – from flopping in front of a TV to meditation on emptying the mind – we are no longer in control of what enters our minds or unconscious. We lose the power to discriminate and so become vulnerable.

Take, for example, listening to music, which many people see as a leisure activity. It has been known for centuries that music affects our state of mind and emotions, and so affects our body. The Persians used music for healing in special hospitals. So did Rudolph Steiner. Much of today's music is extremely stimulating. To listen to this when the mind and body need to recover from effort is, to use a medical term, contraindicated. It is over-stimulation; the mind cannot find peace and quiet. On the other hand, Mozart and Bach bring harmony and lightness, as well as a state of calm and order.

Watching the late-night news fills our minds with concern and misery, and then we go to sleep with these thoughts.

Idleness can also be an enemy of rest and relaxation. If we allow ourselves to wander aimlessly with our thoughts and allow our bodies to stagnate, we are straying towards negative thoughts and ill health. It is the same law which states that without energy everything falls apart. Chaos is a negative state and idleness of the mind and body encourages it.

Happiness, peace of mind and a rested body are essentially energized states. Be active in your thoughts to counter the negative tendency, and if you think of rest and relaxation as recharging, you will see that there is something here to achieve; it is not just a letting go.

● WHEN IS IT NEEDED?

When do we need to achieve balance and harmony within ourselves? The answer is, ideally, all the time.

Recharging ourselves will also depend on the balance and harmony in our lifestyle. This state is achieved with persistence and discipline, for example, to flop into bed in a state of mental anxiety, then just crashing into sleep, is not the best way to recharge. We need to know how to prepare for sleep so that it refreshes us. To come home from work and sit in front of the TV all evening does not make us feel better. It actually makes us feel more stale. We need to plan our leisure so that it is creative and recharges us mentally as well as physically.

All the negative states of emotion drain our energy – 'Don't go to bed with a quarrel' is not just another saying, as our state of sleep is affected adversely by the quarrel. Apathy, that dead state, does not allow us to recharge at all. In order to achieve the state of energy that manifests as a rested body and mind, we must become active against our negative emotions as well as following other disciplines on a daily basis.

We can't relax – why? Because we are in a negative state: emotionally, mentally or physically. Examine your own state. Work out why you have allowed yourself to become so bombarded and overloaded and analyse it, ask yourself what assails you.

Reread the section on Emotion (pp. 13–33). You will understand more clearly what action you can take. If you cannot relax there must be a reason. Find it and face it.

● SHOWERS

At the end of the day, you often come home from work feeling heavy and drained. It is as though you are carrying the work of the day with you. You may even feel your skin crawling after a difficult meeting or with the impact of crowds of people.

There is one foolproof way to rid yourself of this – take a cold shower. Let the water wash you all over. At the same time, use your mind to visualize yourself under a waterfall, with all the freshness and cleansing of nature in its torrent. (We will talk more about the role of visualizing in the next section.)

When you feel you have had enough, get out and dry yourself and put on fresh clothes – your home clothes. By 'feel' we mean your inner feelings, not those of your body. This may seem harsh but you will feel the difference. Do this for three days in succession and you will be able to make up your own mind whether it works or not.

Once you have realized how effective and important this simple discipline is to your whole state of mind and body, you will want to do this every evening.

In the morning, when you get up, take a cold shower. It will invigorate you, clearing the night away and preparing you for the day.

In Germany, over a century ago, the Abbé Kneip founded the practice of hydrotherapy. His book *My Water Cure* describes the findings of a lifetime of practice directing his patients to the healing and restoring powers of water. In modern Germany there are more than a hundred spas offering the 'cure', and programmes of hydrotherapy are taken once or twice a year by millions of Germans. The results and benefits are well-documented.

How much better to introduce a discipline that gives these benefits on a daily basis. No more stale, tired, dead feelings. Experience feeling fresh and clear, energized and therefore recharged.

Our inertia is our enemy: the less you want a cold shower, the more you need one.

PART THREE

Waking Up
To Your Inner World

Becoming Aware

- OUR GOALS AND DREAMS

Goals and dreams cannot be separated. You need to dream, then formulate your goals from those dreams and make them a reality. There are those that fulfil their childhood dreams, those that are talented and reach their goals early in life and are penalized because of their youth, as well as those who lack the courage to make their dreams a reality.

Children are dreamers – they want to be doctors, ballerinas, nurses, and more. What is it that goes wrong? Where does the dream, the goal they so passionately formulated go to?

But it doesn't have to be that way. I would like to tell you about two special friends who were blood brothers (perhaps you also remember what it felt like to cut your finger and touch another who had done the same?). Both were boys of 8 years old and had their imaginations fired by Perry Mason, a fictional TV lawyer who helped the poor.

As a result, one friend vowed to practice law in Harlem, New York. He was unconventional – he always used to wear a woolly cap and refused to wear a tie. The other friend, who also decided to become a lawyer, was as straight as an arrow in flight, and in total contrast, was very conventional in his approach to life.

Both of these boys set out to follow their dreams and because of this conviction did, in fact, realize their goals and become successful solicitors.

I have had the great privilege to know some very talented young people whose dreams did come true. However, they are so often held back with comments such as 'you are too young', 'we cannot trust you', 'your time will come' – time and time again I have heard the same complaint by those who have achieved their goals at an early age.

Those who blatantly slap down the enthusiasm and special achievement of young designers, painters, musicians, and other talented young people, often steal their ideas. I remember a case where an architect designer, without excuse bent over the shoulder of his employee, a brilliant 22-year-old designer, and put his name unashamedly to the novel ideas and design of the young man, claiming them for his own.

Jealousy, it is said, is a green-eyed monster. How many of you who read these lines have found yourself in a similar predicament, being denied personal recognition for your achievements.

James Allen said that, 'A man is literally what he thinks'. All of you who read these words have at some time in your youth dreamt the biggest dreams. All right, there were obstacles to fulfilling them; some seemed insurmountable and I am in no way underestimating the difficulties of making your dreams a reality.

What I am saying is that it is never too late to reformulate your goals: don't give up and just accept your lot as if it were a sentence handed out by life. You are a unique human being endowed with your own unique wisdom, understanding and experience which can be put to good use to formulate your goals. Yes, the door will be slammed in your face at first. Your ideas may be rejected; your goals, if voiced too soon, may be laughed at. But remember, *it's your life!* Fight for your dreams.

So many people feel that their lives belong to someone else. They feel that they have lost control and become puppets with someone else pulling the strings. Many times have I heard people say, 'But if there is a God up there, then why does he not help me in my dilemma?' Well, if there is a God and if he can help, would you know what help you truly want, what the changes are that you want to bring about in your life? The main problem is that we rarely know what we really want.

Life will only give you whatever you'll accept. If you accept being average and ordinary, life will help you to stay that way. The world doesn't owe you anything and nobody is going to tap you on the shoulder and hand you an opportunity. You have to go out there and look for it. Your success will come because of your will to succeed and your total commitment to your ideal.

Don't be afraid to make demands on yourself that go beyond your set limit – those who practise sport will recognize the truth in this.

Your question at this point will be, 'How do I start to reformulate my goals?'

The first step you take is to reassess and analyse your situation. Sit and write down what you like or love in life and then what you want to change.

Face yourself, see what changes you can bring about and stop accepting an undesirable situation.

Retrieve your old dreams and dust them off. While there is breath in your body, it is never too late to change.

In the words of Abraham Lincoln 'Always bear in

mind that your own resolution to succeed is more important than any other one thing'.

Don't self-destruct. Don't be afraid to be different. Don't close your ears to the world and don't give up. Take that first step to a new life.

● LISTENING WITHIN

How many times have you read or heard someone say 'Listen within, listen to your conscience, to that still inner voice that will give you direction on how to live your life and how to overcome its hurdles'?

Mankind throughout the ages has produced what we call the Holy Ones. Through their prophetic utterances, each of these in turn has given and passed on the messages of the beings of light who guide mankind. These Holy Ones set out the rules by which we can live our lives and, in turn, reach the state of a higher being which is dormant within each one of us.

Much has been written on the subject of the quest for enlightenment. Have you ever stopped to think of where these Holy Ones, these philosophers, the Sons of God, received their information? True to their craft and their inspiration, they passed this on to mankind. Each Holy One has, in turn, asked us to listen within to the purest guidance that is our entitlement.

Maybe the time has come when they will now pass on the secret that they have so jealously guarded. The secret is *how* to listen to this inner voice without which the Holy Ones would not have been able to pass on the messages they had been given. Why have they never given us the understanding of how to contact this inner voice? Why have they kept this secret to themselves, the chosen few?

We seek the key that opens the door to this inner

consciousness, the lid of the well that we too as individuals can open. We too can take a cup and drink our fill from the living water of light, of true knowledge, logic and love combined.

Was it because the Holy Ones feared that the key to this inner knowledge and the inner voice would be misused that they never revealed their knowledge? It is true that this is so. But it must be the individual's right to choose of his own free will to follow the darkness or the light within himself.

Do not fear that darkness will guide you. Unless you choose it consciously, you will be guided to follow the light.

Again, there are those who would quarrel with this view but let me tell you that we all have a mentor, an inner teacher, a guardian angel, a being of light who protects us and is totally dedicated to the task of leading us to the point of self-realization, to bring about the harmony and peace for which we pray. Our inner teacher is only too willing to guide us, on a minute-by-minute basis, in our endeavours to live the life we choose.

How do we contact this inner guide, this best friend? This is a question which many have asked who seek the path of inner understanding. Some have waited for a booming voice to give direction and are still waiting after years of meditation and prayer.

You may be asking for inner guidance on a daily basis, not knowing that inspiration is already being given to you every time the need arises within your life. This guidance has been given very simply *through your own voice* which talks to you, admonishes, guides, cajoles, takes away your fears, explains and, with infinite care and tenderness, dedicates itself to your daily encounters with life.

Let us take some very simple examples. As you wake up in the morning, you may hear yourself say, 'If you go back to sleep, you won't have time to have breakfast. Why don't you have a shower and wash away the dreams of the night. You'll feel better.' Or, 'Take a warm jacket, it will be cool today.' Or as you shut your front door and panic for a minute, thinking you have left your keys inside, you hear yourself say 'It's all right. They're in your pocket.'

We spend a great deal of time arguing and going against these very simple instructions, but through practice we will find how much care and love is behind these messages.

Let us go back a minute to those leaders of men. They knew that the voice that spoke to them with their own voice was not their own but the voice of a being that had its abode in a world of light.

You will ask yourself a question at this point: 'Why should such a being be interested in the routines of my daily life? Why should a being care about what time I get up, what I wear, what I eat?'

Again, let me take you back – this time to the moment when you first fell in love. Remember how the face of your beloved was with you in everything you did? Remember how you were concerned for his or her welfare, how you wanted to know if he or she had slept well, had eaten properly or was too cold or too hot? Remember how you would gladly have given your life to have saved his or hers?

Well, look upon your relationship with your friend, your mentor, as just such a relationship and let your mentor guide you throughout your day in everything you do. Nothing is too big or too small for his concern. Listen to the voice talking to you in everything you do and know it is not your voice, but the inner voice of the one who cares for you with love and infinite tenderness.

Let him *prove* his existence to you. Not for a moment do I want you to believe unthinkingly in what I say. Instead, try it out! Gather evidence, on a daily basis, of your guide's existence.

It is necessary and immensely touching that your mentor should take the trouble to give you comfort in every step you take, in a very basic and everyday way. What he wishes to do is to establish through everyday occurrences the realization within you of his existence. Through this you, who have thought that the inner and outer struggle was your own, will understand, know and comprehend through the deepest fibres of your being that you are no longer alone and that everything you do matters to someone.

Let me take some more examples. You need to speak to someone in authority. In the past, when you have approached that person, you felt you had chosen the wrong moment. Now, before speaking to that person, whether your boss or partner, ask your mentor to inspire you and to tell you the right time, to choose the right place and to give you the right words and the correct approach – and to help the other party accept what you have to say.

Other examples might include a routine car journey, when you have a feeling that you should fill up with petrol before the tank is empty. You do so at an unfamiliar garage and then discover that the one you had planned to stop at was closed. You might take an unexpected turning just because it feels right, and discover a lovely place to eat. You might feel a spontaneous urge to buy a particular present for a loved one and then find it has always been their secret wish. Or you might be invited to a party, start to feel uncomfortable and have the courage to comply when your inner voice tells you to go, knowing that your guide will keep you safe from harm.

You see, you must learn to ask for this guidance within on a daily basis. Having asked for very specific things and following the instructions your mentor gives you by speaking with your own voice, you will see the results.

There are two situations, however, where your mentor cannot inspire you with his guidance.

Firstly, if you misuse your free will and seek to gain power over another human being or you act falsely for your own gain and let your own desires blind you. Further, if you ignore the consequences that these actions may have for another, the voice of your mentor will then be replaced by a different voice guided by greed, destruction and hardness of heart.

Your next question will be, 'How do I know which voice I am listening to, because both mentors choose the same voice to speak?'

One, if obeyed, brings harmony, rhythm and immediate peace within, even if this small voice is not what we wish to hear. The other voice often brings immediate reward but takes away the inner light and hardens the heart, blinding us to what is right and what is wrong, so that we are no longer certain which path to take. This is the chatterbox – out-talk it!

Often, you have asked yourself if there is a power out there that is supposed to help when you need it. You have asked why it does not give you what you require. The answer to that is that nine times out of ten you do not know what you really want, you do not know your own mind and have not made a choice.

You are hampered by fear of the consequences of a new choice, the fear of the unknown, of being alone, of rejection if you choose not to continue to be a part of the world you have readily accepted in the past. By not knowing and by feeding these fears, you have played into the hands of the mentor whose dedication is to keep you away at all costs from your higher self and who will feed off your essence and life energy, as without these it cannot live.

Now you have the key to listening within. It is your responsibility and yours alone to choose which voice to listen to, which voice to accept as a guide throughout your daily life. No one can make that choice for you.

You will ask yourself, 'If I listen to my best friend within and follow the precepts, will he lead me to the same holiness as those whose life was dedicated to the light?' The answer is that first and foremost your individual guide is there to help you achieve your dreams and to bring into your life the harmony, peace and love you crave for.

If at any stage you wish to go beyond your daily existence and to ask for the knowledge of how you can reach your higher self, then your guide will teach you about the workings of your mind, your intellect and how to rise from your lower mental being into that of perfection. Your mentor will teach you how to purify your will and liberate your spirit so that ultimately, you can govern your own destiny.

The next sections are for those who wish to reach that ultimate being within, and touch the total freedom of action. These sections will introduce the principles involved, clarifying, explaining and analysing the steps which are necessary to reach that perfection of being. Contrary to belief, this does not lift you out of this world in which you live, but it does allow you to take your rightful place within this world in the totality of your being.

If you do not want that guidance within, that's all right too.

When to do something, when to stop, all these things which are in tune with the rhythm of your life are the result of listening within. All of us, to a greater or lesser extent, have been doing this all our lives. Imagine the joy of our mentors when we recognize what is going on and happily accept and welcome this process. It must be like loving someone from afar only to have them turn to us one day, recognizing the love we have held for them and the secret things we have done for them, and returning our love with their own. What greater joy can there be?

It is a joy to know of the support of our mentor at every stage, to talk to him, to exchange ideas, to consider the next step, in fact, anything at all. What a team. It is the perfect relationship.

● LOVE

'The one thing we all ask for is love. The one thing we all fear is the loss of love. Our one great sorrow is the sorrow of the separation from love and the aim in all our hidden longing is to find love.' (Sri Aurobindo)

There is a need in all of us to find the fulfilment of belonging. We search for the other half, consciously or unconsciously. Yes, the other half does exist, and when it is found the love is eternal and absolute and brings with it a fulfilment of identity. There is no experience of division or isolation because true love has no other motive than love, and the beloved is all that initially concerns us.

All our emotions are harnessed in our endeavour to find true love. Often we are baffled, because having found love it then eludes us; there is no permanence, only loss that leaves us wanting.

True love is not egotistical, self-regarding, full of grief or irresistible demands, afflicted with anger, jealousy or self-satisfaction. Love is not the impure self-seeking that chokes everything in its wake.

In its pure form, love is emotional understanding. It is a close drawing together of two worlds and is there for mutual aid. Love makes concessions and gives mutual support. The only tears which are ever shed are those from actions unwittingly committed which have hurt the beloved.

In true love there is no self-effacement, only self-fulfilment, no mutilation or degradation but transform-ation and transmutation into a mutual higher self where self-expression is one of mutual joy and understanding. This is always gentle and never crude. There is no 'I-ness' and 'My-ness' in love. Love is a foundation of oneness in ecstasy which is pure and sublimated. This brings with it mutual and total devotion.

This is the love we seek. We cry for it in the night, for this perfect union. Figuratively speaking, who would not give their right arm to find such a love?

Love also yearns for beauty. When love is found in its entirety, it represents total bliss. When this perfect love is lost the nightingale no longer sings.

When we fall in love we drop the boundaries that are usually described as our ego. Our consciousness merge, one with the other and for a fleeting moment in time, it touches the unmanifested half in the other, creating an inner union of perfection.

If the attraction was dominated by sexuality then when this flame diminishes, as it so often does, the partners fall back into their own boundaries and wonder where the magic has gone. This is when two people should begin the real act of loving, but they rarely do because it requires effort and commitment.

For some, having experienced the realities of such a love and having lost it, there is total annihilation of the self and a feeling of total abandonment. The nightingale can no longer sing. Others seek but do not find the true love of their dreams. They go from one set of arms to another, hoping to find that lasting union with the beloved.

Some people, and you may be one, slowly and partially pick up their lives after losing their love. They realize, after a painful time of feeling abandoned and finding the courage to analyse their relationship, that it was not all they were hoping for and love was wanting. They find the courage to face their neglect and rejection, and see it as a blessing in disguise to give them, at last, the freedom from the constant humiliation which was apparent during their time together. Marriages, contrary to belief, are not necessarily made in heaven. Having faced life without the departed partner, they can look forward to fulfilling their dream of finding the one who will share their life in a more perfect union.

Others lose their love through the separation of death or divorce and they grieve for the loss of the one who, to all intents and purposes, did share their everyday life and existence. For all the show of outward appearances of being a couple however, perhaps there was no deep abiding love and the one left behind hangs onto a myth of a union that had ceased to exist many years ago. They continue to mourn for years after the death or loss of their love but their loneliness was just as real when their partner was alive.

When the truth of the relationship together is faced, the prospect of living alone suddenly ceases to be unbearable. Analysing the relationship may – and will

– be a painful process but it is also one of healing, for if you can admit to yourself that the relationship was not perfect and was in many ways extremely frustrating, then the sense of loss and abandonment will no longer be as painful. You can start to make a new life for yourself.

How?

Just think for a moment. You could start making your own dreams come true. You always wanted to change those curtains and that carpet in the bedroom. Now you can without being reprimanded. Why not see your Aunt Maude? You lost touch with each other because your partner never got on with her. Ring her up and enjoy the freedom of conversation. Look up old friends you gave up for your partner's sake. Enjoy sitting in a room without the smoke that choked your lungs for years.

On the other hand, if you have lost your partner and like two branches of a tree, you had grown together in kindness and only lived for each other through thick and thin, then talk inwardly to your partner. In your mind, tell them what you are doing and ask for their guidance. Wait for their inner voice and know that you will meet again someday. Remember all your happy times, be creative and do all those things you promised each other you would do together. Live your life with them, in them and through them. Who told you that this could not be?

● DEATH

We are afraid of death. No one wants to talk about it. It is a delicate subject. We have an understandable aversion to bodily cessation.

Religion has taught, to a greater or lesser extent, that we need the cessation of what we call life in order to gain joy, fulfilment, freedom and liberation from our toils and troubles, promising perfect bliss after death.

The field of immortality is discussed at length by all those who have been largely accepted as authorities on the subject. These authorities instill in us acceptance of life in this world and putting all our hopes into the illusion, or non-illusion, of the afterlife. The reality of here and now is so often ignored and with it, the possibility of creating paradise here and now. Look at India, for example, where life is based on non-action. So much emphasis is placed on the afterlife that the conditions of the present life are extremely neglected.

We tend to have a life of total acceptance of the present situation we find ourselves in, immovable precepts often imposed either by our own programming, the weight of tradition or our own fears of change. The feeling that this is how it has to be, that there is no way out, causes us to wear our chains gladly. These are so often fastened by those who, in the name of love, secure our chains daily in case we have any notions of escape. We also secure our own chains, for fear of change.

As long as it does not impinge upon another's needs, get up and fight for your rights, your space and for your needs. Become aware of your infinite consciousness, for nothing is finite. We live within the laws of change. It is you and only you who, by accepting your condition,

create insurmountable walls. Break these walls down –
you have the tools. If you don't, then seek them out.

You fear death, the annihilation of self, but often you
are already dead within. If you have opted for non-
action, then you have opted for a living death. The
force that perpetuates the acceptance of living death is
the negative force. This force is very much alive within
your life because you feed it with your fears.

But why wait. Do your utmost to create a good life
for yourself here and now. The fear of death can stunt
your life – but only if you let it.

Visualization

Once you have begun to understand that recharging yourself is an active and not a passive exercise, the next step is to learn to use your most powerful tool: the mind.

The scientific world is beginning to discover what metaphysical teachers have known for centuries, that our world is not composed of any matter at all and that its basic component is a kind of energy or force.

On atomic and subatomic levels seemingly solid matter is seen to be small particles within particles which eventually turn out to be just pure energy. Things that we perceive to be solid and separate are in reality just various forms of energy.

Many centuries ago the Chinese founded a system of medicine based on this knowledge. Understanding that thought could influence the body for good or ill was part of their diagnostic practice. We can say that we are truly what we think. And if we harness our minds to influence our bodies and our internal blocks we can change our health and attitudes, habits and perception of our own limitations.

It is often stated that we only use 10 per cent of our brain. The missing 90 per cent is where the left-hand brain thinkers would not dream of looking for it – it lies in our capacity to create pictures, to visualize. For by doing so we can change ourselves and thus change the world around us.

Your inner teacher will guide you all the way. As we have stated earlier, practices of meditation which require us to empty our minds are passive and so we are vulnerable. Like life itself, the mind is never still. Even in its most calm state it still resonates to brain waves that vibrate at eight cycles per second.

Using our minds actively to recharge means we can also overcome some of our blocks and limitations. If we understand that our left-hand brain, like a computer, can store images of defeat and inability, then we can see how we need to reprogramme our expectations at a deep level.

Hypnosis has been used to introduce new suggestions to people that will change established programmes. Indeed, it is widely accepted and applied as a technique. Often a tape is purchased, with the hypnotist's voice making new suggestions such as 'you will be relaxed at the start of your next race', or 'when you reach the half-way point in the race, you will find new energy' or 'when you go to the next committee meeting, you will not feel dominated by the others, but will feel free to express your views without fear': the applications of this technique are endless.

However, there is a major drawback. You are letting someone else's voice and energy into your subconscious and as such, are becoming led by another person on whom you are then dependent for your changes and success.

The use of images that are subtly out of tune with our inner world can be extremely damaging and many of the images and practices applied by practitioners can cause new problems while attempting to solve existing ones.

It is far better that you make your own tapes and choose your own images. Just as when reading a favourite novel, we create the people and places described as we see them, so we draw on our own images and imagination to enrich our inner world, rather than accepting an unknown intruder – the voice on the tape.

The 'Inner Game' as this type of work has come to be called, is established in tennis and applied to a wide variety of professional and amateur sports by people wishing to improve their game. The improvements can be both in physical areas such as getting a back-swing right in tennis or in areas of fear or attitude.

Applied to other areas of our lives, images and use of our own tapes can be used to recharge our bodies and minds and accelerate our learning of new and positive attitudes, to know how to feel and act.

● MAKING YOUR OWN TAPE

Equipment required:

1. A small portable tape-recorder on which you can record as well as play back.
2. A tape, record or CD player.
3. Paper and pen.

The idea is to use music and sound as a background. Natural sounds such as the waves of the sea or the singing of birds are even better than manufactured sound. This will help to create the state of deep relaxation in which we are open to the ideas and images we will put on the tape with our own voice.

When we listen to gentle and beautiful sounds, the

vibrations are actually massaging our tissues and cells which, in turn, improve blood circulation, metabolism and hormone action. This is the background against which we can listen to our own suggestions on the tape and change.

Before you begin, remember that you are the product of your thoughts and be aware of what you think.

Read through this section before you start to plan your tape. Just thinking it over, you will see how deep and positive an influence this can be. Write down your words before you speak them into the tape. Use 'I' all the time. It is you speaking to yourself.

Start the music and record one or two minutes to begin the all-important process of deep relaxation.

Say out loud:

My muscles are becoming relaxed, my legs are relaxing, my feet first, then torso. They are feeling light. My abdomen is relaxing, the tension is loosening and a lightness is replacing it.

My chest is relaxing, my breathing is steady and light. My arms are relaxing. First my fingers, then my forearms. A wave of lightness flows up my arms into my shoulders and into my neck. The tension in my neck is easing.

My jaw is loose. My eyebrows are unknotting. My back, from my legs to my head, is light and free. I am totally free and relaxed, all my muscles feel loose, my nerves feel unknotted, nothing can disturb my inner peace.

I feel well. I am calm, quiet within and without, relaxed, free. I feel at ease within myself and I am at peace.

Then tape two to three minutes of music – softly. Your choice of peaceful music to harmonize your inner state of relaxation.

Speak:

In my imagination I create . . .

This place can be used for visualizing yourself in nature. These images that you create can be a great source of healing and recharging. It is a chance to go in your mind to a special place, known only to you, where you can find the peace and serenity you so desperately need. Let me give you some suggestions that will help you to find your own way:

I am on a beach, clean white sand, soft under my bare feet. The soft branches of trees overhang the sands.

It is dawn. Over the ocean, beyond the gently breaking waves, the sun is rising. A new light on a new day. The glow fills the sky from the east until the edge of the sun lifts up above the edge of the ocean. The first rays touch the beach and warm my body.

I feel the growing power of the sun as it lifts into the day. It gives that power to me. I receive it with a grateful heart and let the light enter into me, until I am light. Life is renewed within me.

It is a warm and gentle day as I walk towards the wood that beckons me, cool and friendly. I find the path that leads under the green boughs into its depths. As I pass into the cool, dappled light, the deep silence of the wood surrounds me.

Still and calm, the gentle trees soar around me, sheltering me and sharing my joy and calm. We are brothers, these trees and I, breathing the same air, alive and still. Deep within this wood is my special place.

My heart fills with the anticipation of this perfect grove, towards which I am walking. I am close now. The birdsong alone breaks the silence. As I walk out into the sunlight, the grass is soft under my feet.

The sun's warmth falls on my body, its rays filling me and driving from me all fear and shadows. I am safe within my place of peace.

*

I have come across the meadows to the place beneath the willows, where I will find the brook. I come to its edge and see it cool amongst the rushes, a place of little fish and soft green grass.

I sit down upon its bank and remove my shoes and socks. I roll up my trousers and lower my toes into its chattering surface. The sunlight falls upon the surface of the brook, casting diamonds of light on the ripples. The cool water is around my ankles as I sit on the bank, basking in the warm sunshine.

In my imagination, I can lift off the top of my head, just like a lid. As I do so, a shaft of light comes from above, sparkling with diamonds just like those on the water. As this enters my head, my negativity begins to flow out of the soles of my feet and is taken away by the stream. It is like a cloud of ink swirling downstream.

The light penetrates deeper into me, down my arms, chest, abdomen and finally my legs, until all the grey heaviness has been washed away and nothing remains within me but the sparkling light. I am restored and utterly at peace.

I have a memory, half forgotten from that time of youth and magic, that knows of a secret garden. There is a wall, old and high, covered with vines and jasmine. Great tangled briars hide the ancient brick and stones. Only I know of the old door hidden behind a crumbling shed.

I slip round to where my hand finds the iron handle. It turns with ease and with a light touch, the ancient iron-bound door moves. I slip through and my senses are immediately alive to a new intensity. My eyes have to adjust to a more brilliant light. The birdsong is clearer, the smells of the garden are light and fresh in my head.

As I adjust, I see the most perfect garden, tended by invisible hands with exquisite taste and love. A garden of perfect harmony. My heart tells me of a perfect flower in the centre of the garden and I move along the pathways, stopping to drink in some new and dazzling sight or scent that arrests me.

Turning a corner by a fountain, I see a rose, illuminated in its brilliance. Perched alone in its beauty as if a queen amongst her subjects. From this rose radiates perfect peace and understanding. All thoughts of doubt and shadows fall away from me in the face of this perfection. I approach until I can see the velvet petals arrayed in radial symmetry. The scent makes my head light. An understanding of perfection fills me and I feel a deep humility. The gift of the rose is serenity and love and I, grateful and silent with awe, receive this gift in my heart. Its vibration harmonizes all my thoughts and feelings, as I gaze fixed into the depths of this greatest of flowers.

I feel nothing but my new self: the gift of the rose.

Then switch the music on again, gently. Enjoy the exercise of doing this well, so that a harmony of sound takes over your gentle voice for two to three minutes.

Continue to say:

I feel new strength, vigour and energy entering my being, flowing through me like rivers of light. I have a feeling of total security and protection. When I leave my newfound sanctuary, I will remain calm and peaceful within, taking with me the gifts I have been given.

Everything I do in future I will tackle with total concentration and self-assurance, and I will do it well.

I shall enjoy life.

I will learn to know myself with the help of my inner teacher. I must remind myself that fear and my submission to it is a statement of disbelief. It denies the intervention of my inner teacher on my behalf, because I close the door within and block the light that would dissipate the darkness that angers and frightens me.

Play another one to two minutes of music.

The following text is for self-healing. At this point

you will be renewed, relaxed and ready to reprogramme yourself.

My health is improving from day to day. With every breath
I am allowing the healing energy to penetrate and per-
meate my lungs, heart, liver, kidneys and digestive
organs. I follow the light energy through my muscles, my
bloodstream, renovating every cell. Every fibre of my being
is revitalized through this life energy.

Another one to two minutes of music.
Speak:

I can activate within my unconscious the healing power.

Guided by your inner teacher, then add what you know
you need. The list below will give you some idea of
what you can do. Use these suggestions if you wish.

I am strong and worthy.
I can handle . . .
I am in control . . .
I am active, not passive.
I am loving.
I am worthy of being loved.
I am not a victim. I am taking responsibility for my life.
I will no longer give power over me to anyone else, so
they can sabotage my life.
Enough is enough.
I can direct my own life, plan it and carry it through.
I will not blame anyone else or any outside force in my
life. I am responsible.
I will not expect anyone else to make me happy but will
find it within me.
I will not say if only . . .
I am not a failure. I tried, so I am a success.
Ships in harbour are safe but that is not what they were
built for. They were built for sailing the oceans.

I am breaking through old patterns and moving forward with my life.

I am creating the perfect relationship inspired by the statement 'feel the fear and do it anyway.'

This woman/man is not my life, but if we are meant to be together, we will be. If not, so be it. I trust that my inner teacher and my inner self are creating the perfect relationship for me. I can let go, trusting that everything is happening perfectly.

It is all happening for my growth.

My life is full and rich and there is nothing to fear.

Or:

The work that I find so hard will become easy, for it is my attitude and inner blocks that make such heavy weather of it. These will fade away and I will find joy and enthusiasm for what I do.

Or:

My golf swing is tense and uneven because I am tense and uneven. I will find a rhythm and flow in my body like the swaying of a willow in the breeze. This I will bring to all I do.

Then you can play some more music for as long as you like.

When you have understood the gist of this and talked to your inner teacher about what you need as an individual, you will be able to sit down with paper and write your own script.

One ninety-minute cassette gives you forty-five minutes on each side which is enough for most people. When you have done the recording, you can listen to it whenever you have time to spare; before you go to bed, first thing in the morning, or whenever suits you.

As your needs change and you grow, your inner

teacher may tell you that some points need changing on your tape. This is fine.

You can enjoy the feeling that you and your life are moving in the right direction towards action, health, harmony and independence.

The Perfection of Self

- **PSYCHOLOGY**

Following the Renaissance, the Age of Reason produced a rational view of the world through philosophy
and science. In many ways this was a reaction to the
centuries of domination by the Church with its demand
for faith alone as the understanding of life. The teachings of the Church brought nothing tangible for mankind.

Rational philosophy explored the human condition
without the element of spirit. Indeed Descartes, in the
seventeenth century, argued that the mind and body
were separate material things. As science progressed,
so medicine followed producing a medicine of the
mind; psychology. A science distinguished by its complete lack of the spiritual element in its understanding
of human life; just as its predecessor, the Church of the
Middle Ages, had denied mankind its reason.

The process of psychology tends to offer a denial of
personal responsibility in life; no space is given for the
truth of the soul's own choice of its own learning and
need for experience and atonement. The subject is often
shown how to pass the blame for his or her own problems in life onto others – be they parents, teachers or
environment. Therefore they do not learn to solve their

own problems through an awareness of the process of spirit.

By the process of psychology the subject is all too often bound to the negative events in their lives and focuses on the negative results in their personality. Being encouraged to resent what has often been the well-spring of their humanity, they cannot grow from the experiences by accepting the inner scars as evidence of their worthy struggle to overcome themselves.

So psychology often binds us to our weaknesses and failure by showing us how to 'pass the buck' and so makes us believe that we should feel good when we have done so. It excuses our own behaviour.

The relationship of client and therapist can even be a psychic cannibalism where the therapist preys on the pain and emotions of the victim. A 'come into my parlour' situation that is perpetuated, often for many years, until there is nothing left to 'dig out', whereupon the client is either cured or given drugs to keep them quiet. The process of psychology can become like a drug with the victim as addicted to their own helpless indulgence as the therapist is to the emotional charge that they get. The victim is given in return, by seeing the cause of suffering as being outside themselves and identifying it, instant absolution for their past, present and future behaviour. The antithesis of what Buddha taught.

It must be said that because, traditionally, psychology comes from a denial of spirit whoever goes into the process is cut off from their own light. Whereas by welcoming the light within themselves and by taking responsibility for their own karma, they can become relieved of the burden of self-delusion that blocks the gift of awareness. Our western understanding of consciousness differs from that developed in the East in one major way.

In the West, we search outside ourselves for the source of inspiration, creation and truth. In the East, they have made this journey inside. In the West, we blame the external world for our problems. In the East, they have understood the need to put their internal world in order.

The eastern journey is more intuitive, open and capable of holding contradictory concepts without confusion. The western way is more linear, logical and rational. This is a reflection of the left and right sides of the brain contained within one human being.

We can blend the two, without prejudice, to provide the stepping-stone for a more complete psychology. Ordinary psychology only takes the mind and its working at surface value. It does not help us on a path of self-exploration and self-conversion.

We can aspire to a higher consciousness. We can free our spirits, throwing away our limitations, our bonds and our obscuring confusions which we have brought about ourselves.

The idea that thought is the highest human quality is part of our inheritance. It is accepted that what separates us from the other creatures sharing our planet is our capacity to think. The measure of our thinking is often the performance of our intellect. This is a reflection of the internal world in which we live. Emotions, fears, doubts, are all processed and appear as thoughts which are not under our control.

The intellectual mind is the product of the brain and the initiator of thought but its passion for analysis and argument often ends up shedding confusion, rather than light, on any subject. Often the brain does not find the answer, but produces more unanswerable questions, behaving like a washing machine with too much of the wrong soap. It overflows with bubbles which are our thoughts. To get it to work properly, we have to clear out the old powder, which are our old conditioned thought patterns, and replace them with the right ones.

Hidden behind this limited intellectual mind is a mind of pure wisdom with an affinity for clear understanding, well-known in the East. From our contacts with it, we call it our intuition, our creative source, the unfathomed well of inspiration, the genius and the unexpected.

All our limitations are bound up in our intellectual mind with its boundaries and imperfections and its tendency to emotional distortion. By clearing out this mind and asking for help from our mentor with our intuitive self, which is hidden inside us, we can progressively strengthen ourselves.

Yet we experience a great sense of loss, if we only let go of this intellect reluctantly and in fact would rather nurture it than shed it. Into this negativity goes all the support for our minds and all the arguments it needs to strengthen the intellect and to give it reasons not to shed its skin.

This is the greatest challenge of all. The highest achievement a human being can aspire to is to become centred in the intuitive mind, guided and supported by our inner teacher and listening with an aware and practised inner ear.

As with all great adventures and challenges, the rewards and achievements are not handed out on a plate. We have to accept the disciplines and the degree of awareness and honesty required.

To know yourself is to become master of your own ship. To gain that knowledge means we must not be afraid of what we may uncover within our nature in this process of self-analysis. This has been the aim of a large part of mankind's intellectual and moral striving but it is our self-awareness and not intellectual procrastination which is the key that opens the door to the self.

We have to stop accepting habits and limiting conditions of our present life and start to observe our actions and reactions to situations.

Begin by watching yourself for half an hour each day as if you are a stranger. Pick different times and learn to observe and then analyse your behaviour and reactions: how do you greet the man in the newsagent? how do you address an acquaintance at work? how do you behave towards your superiors and your subordinates at work?

You are in for some surprises. Observe also how you behave at home.

You will become aware that you are not always what you want to be. You need to work on yourself, to strive towards perfection of your self. This is not an unattainable ideal, but a goal which you must pursue in order to avoid stagnation.

● FREE WILL

What is this free will that we say is such a vital part of our lives? We claim that it is our right, and yet, so often, in so many little things, our free will is guided not by our relationship with our inner friend, but by our selfish, greedy nature.

So before you exercise your free will without thought, weigh up and be aware of the consequences of using your free will. Ask yourself the question, 'Is it my desire, my greed, my wish to be in control that drives me in this matter, or do I feel the lightness of purpose that is a mark of the guidance from within?'

If it is your passion that is in the driving seat, ask yourself whether you care what effect the actions of your free will will have upon others or upon yourself. Are you prepared to carry the pain and suffering that you may cause by exercising your will, if it is a selfish act?

Even in your decisions, you find you are often in turmoil and do not know where to turn. You feel you have tried all ways, listened to advice, thought about your life but still cannot see your way clear. You know you have to do something but are unclear and afraid of the first step.

The first thing to do is to ask yourself what you truly want. Most of the time we do not know the answer to that clearly. Often, we seem to be spoiled for choice and hampered, even paralysed, by our fear of the unknown. This is the time to use your free will. Free will allows you to choose which road to take in life.

One way will ensnare you and entangle your life to such an extent that you will find it difficult to extract yourself from the situation in which you suddenly find yourself. This is when free will has again been used for egotistical desires, your need for power, riches, or a soft ride. If you choose this road, your energies will be consumed by the negativity that you and no one else have unleashed. You will find no happiness, for ultimately life does not allow you to get away with anything, but rather, it has an uncanny way of asking for payment when we least expect it.

On the other hand, we can choose to use our free will for inner and outer growth, to bring about change that does not impinge upon another's space. In this endeavour, we can ask for guidance within. Having used our free will in this way, we will find new energy arising, new strength and vigour, and new ideas flourishing from nowhere. New joys and new opportunities will arrive which we have never dreamt of.

So, stop walking through life with a stubbornness of heart, shutting out your awareness of the consequences of your words, thoughts and actions.

Be aware and choose.

● A NEW BEGINNING

Look into your heart. Ask yourself what it is that you can change. Have the courage to look at your thoughts and your actions. Be steadfast and make a pledge to yourself that you will no longer compromise in any way.

You need to develop certain qualities to raise yourself out of your present state: be honourable in your dealings with others and only speak the truth which is in your heart. Do not disguise your intentions in order to achieve your own ends as doing this only feeds the negativity within you. If you fall into this trap, it will be your own doing – and your undoing. Deceit only brings shame. If the spirits of truth and deceit struggle in your heart, and you choose deceit, then you must take the consequences of your actions. Do not place the blame anywhere but on yourself, because you alone have chosen that path. Further, do not expect to be rewarded. Rather, learn from your actions and then choose the path which will lead you to inner peace and self-respect.

If you transgress, go back to the beginning of your intent and start again. Aim for a newness in your life – think of yourself as newly born, you have no past, no present, no future. Decide from that moment that, unless what you touch gives harmony and peace within, you will leave it alone.

In most cases you do not need to change your environment or what at present is your life or your job. You need to look at others with new eyes, to look at the people within your home and at work in a different way. Ask yourself what you can do to ease their burdens? Stop expecting anything from them.

The world owes you nothing: you owe the world. Do not expect the world around you to change. It is you, in your newness, who will bring about the change. Watch how you can make a difference to your environment. Make a new start.

Tell yourself, 'The very fact that I am alive gives me the right to a new beginning.' It is you who can make the difference at the office by distributing a little kindness instead of putting all your energy into your expectations of others. Put your energy into bringing about changes in your life.

The disciplines will be a daily reminder of the possibilities of newness that *you*, and no other, can create in your life. Perfection seems one of the hardest things to give out. Nevertheless we crave it and would do anything for it. Wouldn't we do anything for a loved one to take us in his or her arms?

Try something. When coming home from work after a heavy and demanding day, take your partner in your arms and watch his or her reaction. They may look at you and say, 'What is the matter? Is something wrong? Have you lost your job? Has the Bank Manager been at you again?' So unaccustomed may he or she be to the affection that you offer.

In the past, your affection would not have ended in a hug and the giving of warmth to each other. The acceptance of that affection would have automatically given that partner the right to carry it further into the realm of sex, where so often, so little affection is given.

When did you last, after such a hug, instead of taking your partner to bed, take him or her by the hand and walk into the garden? Talk of how you have missed them, instead of letting loose an avalanche of words about all that has gone wrong that day? When did you last look at the stars together?

You may wish for a partner to give you all that, but what are you prepared to give of yourself?

● START AGAIN

Go back to the moment when you first met and remember how it felt. Talk about the dreams you had together for the future.

It is not your partner that needs changing. In most cases, it is you who has lost the way, enmeshed in the currents of life.

The demands made upon you are not belittled. The pressure of work, the need to earn, the pressure of family and children, the disappointment of new partners are only too real but do not say, 'I only have strength to carry on this path I am treading. I don't have time for all this rubbish.'

Force yourself to take a day off. Walk along a river, sit by the sea, stroll through the woods and start to analyse the components and blockages that make up your present existence. It is you and no other – and this will be repeated again and again – who can start to make the difference. Try it and see.

When you change the behaviour pattern which has become second nature to you, the world around you will react differently. Fear of change, of newness, is feeding the negativity within you. It is perpetuating its independent existence within your being, taking away your ability to control your life because you have handed this over to your lower nature – or to 'life' – within you. This is not to be desired but analysed. You let yourself be whipped by the fears that assail your mind and paralyse your actions.

Look back to the section on Fear (pp. 26–30). Try to stand up and demand that fear leaves your inner being, like an unwanted guest. If a thought connected to fear bombards you, visualize the object of fear in front of a solid oak door and slam the door in its face. Watch how your own breath will come back into your body. Watch the difference it will make to your life.

By shutting this door to exclude fear, even if you have to do it a million times, you are making the statement that you decide not to let that thought feed on your life's energy. If initially you find this is too hard to do, see the reason why this time you are afraid to shut the door. For instance, if you speak about one you love who has betrayed you, you are afraid that if you shut the door on that person they will never come back and find the love which is between you both.

Understand that you are not shutting the door on the one you loved, but you are shutting it on the negative force that lived – or still lives – within them. While you live, there is hope; while he or she lives, there is hope. Life without hope is a living death.

You can have a mentor, call it whatever you will as semantics are irrelevant here. Call upon that mentor, that inner being of light we all have within us, to help you become active within your present life.

Shutting the door makes a statement of refusal. It also allows you to start a newness within your mind which was hitherto filled with the pain of loss and the pain of the control you had given to another to live

your life. This may not always be on a personal level –
it could be in your work when you make an inner stand
refusing to accept what is dished out to you by shutting
that inner door. You free yourself of the hold others
had over you when *you* allowed them this control over
your life.

Stand up and say, 'This is my life. It is within my
power to change it.' Refuse the control that others seem
to have over you. By closing this door a million times
to your fears, you will gain the strength to create newness in your life.

Remember also that you are not alone. You have your
mentor. Please read the section on Listening Within
again (pp. 58–64). Know that you are loved and that
everything you do matters to your mentor and, ultimately, to yourself. You owe it to yourself to extract
yourself from your present situation and reassess your
life.

It is only when you take the courage to look at yourself and your life – without judgement, without prejudice – that you can decide to make it a new life. Stop
looking outside yourself. There is no one that will give
you the keys to paradise. It is you, having shut the
door on your fears which have hitherto ruled your life,
who can open a new door.

The first step is the hardest. Imagine that when you
come home from a holiday, your house has been taken
over by squatters. What would be your reaction? Would
you welcome them with open arms? Or would you tell
them in no uncertain terms to leave immediately?

Look upon your inner self as your home. You have
allowed squatters to live within you. Now tell them
firmly to leave your inner sanctuary. Cleanse your inner
self of the forces, coupled with fear, that push you out
of your inner sanctum.

Say '*Enough is enough*' . . .

'The soul of man is a world full of beings, a kingdom in
which armies clash to help or hinder a supreme conquest.
A house where the gods are our guests and which the
demons strive to possess.'

Sri Aurobindo

● ALPHA AND OMEGA

What is life about? Where am I going? Who am I? These
are questions that man has asked himself since time
began. There are answers and even if these are not
complete, they give us clues to our existence. Life is
experience. From experience comes knowledge. From
knowledge comes understanding. With understanding,
all things are possible.

There are two types of understanding. One comes
from revelation and inspiration, and is guided by a light
higher than the light of human understanding, and a
truth deeper than the truth of outward existence and
accepts a changing reality that ultimately leads to freedom. The other is based on belief; belief that is fixed in
time, defined, indisputable and finite. By its very
nature, it attracts the forces wishing to use its adher-
ents. Inspired by 'his belief', man becomes a pawn in
the hands of other men, gods and demons. He fights
in the battle between the powers of light and darkness
on the side of his choice. Thus, both camps, invisible
to man, use him to materialize their battles and man
becomes the living sacrifice.

Dear reader, please question deeply the validity of
your belief. Ask yourself if your belief is founded on
sufficient data – do not just accept it. However, for this
you need right thinking and a right understanding,

because it is this thinking impulse and action of the higher truth that ultimately leads to inner freedom.

Lay your pipelines to give yourself access to the clear light of understanding, through prayer and guidance from within. There is no short-cut. Man has to go through his personal exploration and final mastery of his inferno. Sooner or later man is shaken out of his unconscious state and is led to his ultimate awakening.

Even the one who has betrayed the light sooner or later is forced to come back to the centre of stability, where he is raised once more into the understanding of clarity and purity of thought and action.

What is the goal of that journey? It is to reach a position where we are no longer assailed by doubts and uncertainties, where we know who we really are and where we are going. We are guided not by fears and desires, but by an inner knowledge that is ours by right of battle. For this is not a journey of peace and tranquillity but a struggle requiring constant effort and application. It calls for the qualities of a fighter, for only with those qualities can we win through the constant traps and barriers laid by the forces that would block our path and drag us down. Only by having fought every battle and won can we be free from the constraints of being used to act out the wheel of life and be truly ourselves.

● PATHS TOWARDS THE LIGHT

Both the West and the Orient have developed, over the centuries, their own mystical traditions, techniques and paths to self-growth.

Thus we find the same teaching in Hinduism, Buddhism, Zen, Taoism, the sacred book of Zoroastrianism and in Islam of which Sufism becomes the perfection.

In the mysteries of the temples of Ancient Egypt and in Greece where the teachings were called the Hermetic Gnosis. In Judaism, where we find the same secret teachings in the Kabbalah. Ultimately we witness how, as Rudolph Steiner described, 'the spiritual deeds of Rama, Krishna, Hermes, Pythagoras and Plato culminate in the unification of all these impulses in Christ'.

At the turn of the century we find a revival of these teachings in Blavatsky's theosophy, Rudolph Steiner's anthroposophy, and Alice Bailey's Arcane School. There are also the teachings of important figures such as Gurdjieff, Krishnamurti and others.

We can also find answers in the teachings of the Rosicrucians and the pure teachings of the Freemasons, in alchemy and in the symbolism found in mythology.

'Seek and you will find, knock and the door will be opened.'

Good Luck.

Index